Mary had Stretch Marks

Mary had Stretch Marks

Tears of sadness, tears of joy

Miriam Connor

Matador
9 Priory Business Park
Kibworth Beauchamp
Leicestershire LE8 0RX, UK
Tel: (+44) 116 279 2299
Fax: (+44) 116 279 2277
Email: books@troubador.co.uk
Web: www.troubador.co.uk/matador

ISBN 978 1783060 382

British Library Cataloguing in Publication Data.
A catalogue record for this book is available from the British Library.

Typeset in Adobe Garamond Pro by Troubador Publishing Ltd
Printed and bound in the UK by TJ International, Padstow, Cornwall

For Brenda and my Mum

CONTENTS

CHAPTER 1

Clean truth

My husband died in 2001. What I miss most was captured during our last moments as Shay drifted into a coma. We had spent the previous two years doing everything we could to stop this from happening but here it was. We looked into each other's eyes, wanting to be wrong but both of us sensing that this might be it. We started grinning. It wasn't a 'let's pretend everything is okay' grin. It was the sort of smile that thrilled parents share over a new born baby's head. The air around us felt as though we were on a beach on a clean fresh day. All the years of daring to 'show up' in the relationship had blown our terror away. Lots of fears were wrapped up in getting to this moment but we landed in the deep peace that comes with being completely seen and loved by another person.

From our first meeting we had trusted that honesty was our best chance to get to grow old together. There is no 'neat' way to do that. Our connection wasn't always pretty but it had always been about being true. It was the one element that we had any power over. When Shay was diagnosed we had tried ranting and railing against death but it still came. Faced with our worst fear it was tempting to pretend that this wasn't happening, to stick our heads in the sand. Deep down we knew that if we chose the ostrich approach, when we came up for air, Shay would be gone. Instead, we held each other's gaze. The connection felt complete, there was nothing left unsaid.

Shay's death has left me hungry for more of the same sort of connection and with little tolerance of anything that feels like bullshit. Losing Shay creates an added pressure in trying to make sense of our lives. If my children had to face something happening to me, who or what could they turn to for solace? Is there something I can do to help prepare them to cope for the times when grief might rip through their hearts? When Shay was here we shared the load; the children were our priority. Alan (Shay's son from his previous marriage) was seventeen, Brian was five years and Grace was two years old when Shay was carried away from us in a box.

Twelve years later: my job description is to feed, clothe and embarrass teens. My son grins that he is immune to me embarrassing him. That sets the benchmark higher. It's a fun challenge that distracts me for a moment from the fact that I am not as complete as I thought I would be, back when I was his age looking to the future. I was sure that I would be more sorted than this by now. I grudgingly accept that the guidance I had growing up was all that was on offer. But I want something that works better for us now. To be inspired by a vision that can carry us through any challenges ahead. Where do I begin to look for that sort of wisdom? What I was taught as a child was intended to prepare me for life. It didn't come close.

My introduction to finding 'truth' was Irish Catholicism. I am still recovering. My teachers meant well, they believed that they were laying a foundation of peace and joy. What they shared was their truth but there was something that felt sticky and heavy about it. There's a lighter feeling when I think that Mary probably had stretch marks. I have no wish to upset anyone by being disrespectful; it is simply because the words feel true in my body. Whenever I feel that easier light feeling, there is a good chance that I am close to what is true for me. I love that.

As a child I was often in trouble for asking questions. I kept hearing contradictions in what we were being told. I couldn't be sure if the message was the problem or if it was me. The nuns were confident that it was me. I fancied the end product of happiness that they were offering but I seemed to be missing an ingredient to be able to make it happen. That's why I love the clarity to discern when truth feels clean or not. It gives me hope that I have the tools needed to make my own version of a good life no matter what happens. All I have to do is pay attention whenever I sense this easier, happy feeling in response to whatever is being presented as truth.

Friendship seems like a good place to find more of it. Belly-laughing friendship where I am accepted and loved for being real about who I am. It encourages me to dare to be more. We don't need to agree. I don't have to like what someone says to have confidence that what I am hearing is their truth. I find great peace there. If something feels like a contradiction we can look at it rather than pretend that it is not an issue, landing straight back into the clean place of true friendship. You know the exquisite feeling of catching up with a cherished pal, hugging hello. The joy of landing in the arms of someone who believes you are enough. The only 'change' they want for you is anything that brings you happiness. In those precious moments, I aspire to being the best that I can be. I trust that I make good choices. I believe that I can be more. It's time for me to make the something 'more' happen.

My first step is to stop automatically hiding when I meet people. I notice strangers on a bus or at a school meeting, anywhere. It matters to me that we have more in common than we dare to show. What stops us getting to a place of real friendship from the outset? For me it is fear of humiliation. Experience has made me wary of showing too much of myself so I presume to hold everything in, unless I feel exceptionally safe. Blending in seems to make better sense. So I sit on the bus looking like a middle aged Mum. I appear house trained, reasonably sane. I care that we are all putting energy into hiding our less than perfect bits from each other.

I don't need anyone to expose themselves but it would be great if we could relax more. It's not about some big reveal. It's about feeling safe, making it safe for each other. Honest friendship is not about saying what we think is wrong about another person. It's about daring to show up in honesty about ourselves. I suspect I would get thrown off the bus if I approached passengers inviting them to relax, reminding them that we all have bits we hide. I figure the only way to find like-minded people is to risk being real myself. To see who jumps up to race off the bus or who dares to stay. That is what this book is about: risking, reaching out to potential friends or to old pals in a fresh way. Sharing insights based on experience rather than theories or ideals. It's less about sharing wounds and more about sharing the solutions we have found. Recycling insights, hoping friends can learn from us instead of everyone having to learn the hard way.

Sometimes it has been easier for me to be honest with a complete stranger than my closest friends and family. I love friendships where I don't have to work so hard to hide my human bits. There is great peace there. Writing this is my search for fresh ways to connect to that peace. I need to take baby steps, to gently consider one issue at a time. I'd love some company. We may not find answers but at least we can dare to be real about the questions. The following is an 'I'll show you mine if you show me yours' but in a decidedly one-sided form. I'd love to hear what works for you and where you found it. This book is an invitation to dare to speak truth to strangers, to soften the edges of our worlds when we come together. I offer you a glimpse of my truth, as clean as I can make it.

CHAPTER 2

The last birthday party

The night Shay died, he had fought hard all day. Several times, when I asked him "is this it?" he replied that he felt strong. In the evening, when he seemed to have drifted into a coma, I contacted the Renal Registrar. She was always very helpful but could only offer that since Shay had defied science often, there was no predicting. His body might simply be in 'resting' mode. Shay had lived past five 'die by dates' already. I phoned Alan to come. While we were waiting, I brought Brian in to see his Dad. My own Dad had died the month before, I had been very conscious of the contrast of his chest rising and falling and then silent. Brian was almost six years old. Holding his hand, I brought him into the room chatting about how breath makes our chest move. I hoped that this would help him to prepare for a time when his daddy's chest wasn't moving. I sat Brian up on my knee, we turned to Shay. His chest wasn't moving. Our Shay was gone.

Two years earlier, a few days after Shay had been diagnosed; a neighbour came over to our car when Brian and I were heading home from the shops. Winding the window down, we had a quick catch up. In passing she spoke of having been to a mutual friend's funeral. As I drove away, I felt cushioned by the warmth of her support. Then Brian's little voice broke through from the back seat:

"What's a funeral, Mammy?"

My brain was mush; I was still in shock from the diagnosis. I clamoured around to find some sort of adequate answer. Our eyes connected through the rear view mirror.

"It's a last birthday party love".

After a pause he asked with that wisdom of wee ones,

"Will we have balloons?"

"Yes, love, I promise we will have balloons".

So, while we all fought to help Shay beat the cancer, we embraced the possibility that we might be celebrating his last birthday party sooner than we felt it was meant to happen.

Birthdays are big in our household. Our emphasis was less on 'last', more on the 'birthday' bit and what Shay loved. He was clear from the outset: no black, no wreaths, lots of music and laughter. He loved roses and fancied the idea of pals pinching a rose from a garden en route to the funeral. Planning the birthday gave him the chance to be a part of what might carry the kids through an unthinkable time, allowing us to chat openly with them. Sometimes we would release some of the pain inside by getting ridiculous in our fantasies of options. Every good funeral has a helicopter and a dump truck at least... By Shay taking ownership of what he wanted and the fact that it was his journey, it was less threatening for all of us. Our story ended in an unhappily ever after, but we made some fabulous memories by not sitting around waiting for that end.

I loved having the privilege of laying him out as he had died at home. Chatting my farewells to him, tenderly moving his now pain-free limbs. Death is abrupt. Laying him out felt like one last gentle hug. The next morning, Shay was removed from the house for a few hours to be embalmed. It was a requirement because he'd had chemotherapy. The kids presumed that it was time to help make the party happen. We went to the funeral home to pick the coffin. Grace desperately wanted a pink coffin. She kept pulling at curtains, looking behind corners, searching for the perfect hue. She was disgusted that there wasn't even a purple one (which was our compromise pink). The funeral director understandably thought that her two year old stomping was a distraught child picking up on the tension. Grace wanted the very best for her Daddy; in her world that was pink. She was furious at the man for being so inadequately prepared. We settled on the one suitable for cremation. Brian liked how that would be Daddy's favourite one anyway because it was the only one with wooden handles.

Grace was appeased that our next task was to find the birthday cake. Brian and Grace had agreed that it would be a Tweenies cake. Grace had graciously conceded that the cake did not have to be pink because Daddy was a boy. Shay felt so close because his courage to discuss these things meant that he was a part of it. Using complementary medicines meant that Shay had taken minimal analgesia, allowing him to remain alert until the end. His favourite way to spend any spare energy was to read with the children or watch a video. In

Grace's world, Daddy's number one TV show was Tweenies too. While we were out picking the coffin, a pal had made a stunning 'Shay's last birthday party' poster. The roses began arriving. Hundreds. In Ireland, we have the tradition of the Wake. The family can choose to have their loved one at home until the night before the funeral. A Wake is friends and family coming together to keep vigil. We cry, laugh and cry as often as needed. Lots of cups of tea or something stronger, sandwiches and fruitcake. Hours upon hours of fond reminiscing, allowing the shock of the death to settle. Having the person at home, where it is familiar to love them, gives us a chance to say proper last goodbyes in our own time. We figured Shay wouldn't know what to do in a church overnight so we kept him at home for the four nights right up to the final service.

At first, Shay being dead worked great for the little ones. No more Daddy disappearing to dialysis for hours or them being shuffled out of the room because Daddy was too tired. They were chuffed to have my full attention at the same time as having Daddy seemingly sleeping nearby. In that toddler mode of waking early and loving being busy, Grace organised picnic breakfasts to have beside him. Grace beamed as she perched on a stool on one side of the coffin with me on the other. We would do a 'cheers' over Shay's body, including Daddy in our picnic. Deep down we didn't believe it was happening. We wanted to find a way to stop this, to rewind back to the day before when our future included Shay. It was very tempting to put Shay into a bed on return from the funeral home. But a coffin was the truth of the situation and a step towards accepting that his body was just a shell now. At the wake, Grace and her pals played chasing using the coffin as den. This wasn't a corpse, this was her Daddy.

The church and crematorium were close to the house. It felt precious to us having the option to walk behind Shay's hearse even though we were in a city. Gracie perched on my shoulders, her little legs kicking, Brian's hand in mine. I was dressed in a colourful mishmash, no black, my Einstein hairstyle testament to the intensive nursing of Shay for the previous two months. None of us were ready to say goodbye, we numbly accepted that it was time.

Shay had picked the music and readings for the funeral. A song for each of us, tunes that he had sung to us when he had held us in hugs. It made him feel close by. In the final planning, I realised that something more was needed. At the Wake a good friend absent-mindedly started humming the Billy Connelly song 'Crematorium': "And for a dollar you can hire a band that'll sing, come on baby light my fire..."

It was perfect. The crematorium filled with hearty guffaws on the day, along with some buttocks-tightening in the pews. Shay would have loved it. Alan spent hours of the wake sitting with a guitar beside the coffin mastering Shay's song choices; he played most of the music live along with his cousin and two of Shay's best mates, Brian and Anne. Declan, another great friend, put people at their ease by doing compere. It was the biz.

CHAPTER 3

What does hope look like?

Two years earlier we had been faced with a choice: to be crushed by Shay's terminal diagnosis or we could dare to hope. We chose hope. Shay dared to hold on to being a daddy and a husband rather than buy the medics' suggestion that he was soon to be a corpse. Doctors call our sort of hope 'false hope' but we found that any hope makes it easier to breathe. We figured that this was a good thing. Our goal was to grow old together so we started one day at a time. Suddenly we smelt the roses without trying. We had more joy in our lives than friends whose biggest challenge was to decide what to cook for dinner. We knew this because we had more joy than we'd had ourselves only weeks before. Now the prospect of bugging each other in old age seemed the equivalent of a lottery win.

Hope for us became like jumping out of a plane, skydiving. For me the image of skydiving works because we had a baseline of terror all the time while we were smiling. When we got over the terror of jumping, we found ourselves holding the kids hands in a circle, flying through the air laughing, exhilarated. It took courage to break free of the inconceivability of Shay dying. Hope meant looking at all possibilities straight in the face. The challenge of hope is that there are no guarantees. When Grace was a toddler, her tendency was to grab. We would suggest that she ask nicely if she wanted something. She would concede, asking "may I have..." but would implode if the answer was no. For her it was enough to ask the question. We would then try to explain that her version wasn't asking, it was telling. Hope means daring to ask, even if the answer is disappointing.

Shay's Dad had died when he was young. It mattered to Shay that his children have a different experience to the one he had when his father died. If he couldn't be there for the kids, he wanted to teach them not to be afraid; to dare to step into life, or even death. We had lectured Alan as a teen that it was about 'wanting what you have, rather than having what you want'.

Now we were facing this head on, it was difficult to swallow. A poster that I had in the seventies suddenly hit home. "If you are not busy being born you are busy dying".

Daring to hope blew a hole in our fears, it threw open the window for fresh air to come in. It's not about being deluded; it is being open to all the possibilities. For me it is to resist deciding the outcome, staying with the question. With so much at stake it was hard work. Children are naturally hopeful, trusting life until proven otherwise. When something that can feel 'hopeless' happens, they look to adults for a map of this scarier version of the world. They can tell when smiles of encouragement are genuine; it is a fine balance to show them how to be upbeat and remain realistic at the same time. There was no way of knowing if we were getting it right, it was a white knuckle ride.

Hope needs fresh energy to feed it. When Shay was in isolation following chemotherapy, I brought new pictures of the kids from a photo booth (this was before phones had cameras) to place on his locker each day. It reminded Shay that we were committed to him always being a part of our lives. Shay found that when all he had beside him was his favourite photo, he fluctuated between daddy pride and searing pain at what he would be missing if he died. Up to date photographs shifted the energy, it helped him to feel the fun of our lives. Some of them were in dress up or making silly faces, reminding Shay that past the door of his isolation room we were ready to play with him. The word cancer made us feel helpless. Choosing to do anything, no matter how small, reminded us that we didn't have to be defined by it.

We dared to ask what else is possible. Sweet moments fed this. One day I got a 'final' call from the hospice, urging me to come soon. I drove like a maniac. I heard myself screaming at the heavens. "Not now, please, please not now." I arrived to what looked like a corpse with sound effects. Shay was down to less than eight breaths a minute. He was making that death rattle sound. His temperature had dropped below normal. His skin was yellow and waxy. Our homeopath had given us a remedy for an emergency like this. I placed the tiny pill through Shay's cracked lips.

The doctor came to help us prepare for the end.

"Shay, you understand that you are dying."

To both the doctor's and my surprise, Shay responded with a weak but quirky grin.

"Nah, I don't think so, not today".

It was Friday, 4.30pm. Understandably the doctor wanted to get home for the weekend before the traffic. With some urgency he repeated how Shay needed to prepare himself. Shay's grin became stronger.

"Not today Doc".

The Doctor looked to me for some hope of a sane response. Shay's grin was contagious.

"I'm with him. He's pulled this stunt more than once."

Shaking his head, the Doctor left us, something about his shoulders speaking his conviction that we were deluded. His truth was that there would be another patient in this bed by Monday.

Monday arrived. Shay had recovered enough to get about in a wheelchair. As we came around a corner of the hospice corridor laughing and chatting, we looked up to the shocked face of the doctor. His genuine surprise was delicious. We grinned and nodded hello. The doctor's reaction shot a bolt of energy and self-belief through Shay's body which fed him for months. In the journey from diagnosis, Shay's confidence increased. If a Doctor tried to tell him this was the end, Shay would say respectfully "Only God knows when my time is up."

We loved the way it shifted our relationships with the medics. It gave them permission to be human too; we didn't need them to have all the answers. Shay would ask them to resist giving him any 'die by dates'.

He'd explain "If I like you enough, I might just try to prove you right".

Shay had always been naturally quiet but he figured he had too much to lose if he didn't speak up this time. His health was in his and God's hands, whoever or whatever that meant for him. The rest of us were extras on the set.

What worked for us was making time for the feelings we wanted to avoid the most. Shay knew what it had taken for him to grieve when his mum had died. So one evening in the hospice, he organised for us to watch Philadelphia, Schindler's List and Shadowlands back to back. It was like having a good crap. Our tears washed away some of the paralysing fear. Breathing was easier for days after that. So whenever we needed to let the lid off our terror, we arranged a 'movie night in' that flushed away any blockages to our daring to hope. It also meant that by the time the funeral arrived, Shay and I had shed our tears together. It left me free to focus on what the children needed because I had cried a river in Shay's arms. There would be plenty of time for tears again when everyone was gone; when it would slowly dawn that Shay was gone too.

Shay left another legacy of his love by setting the example that it is okay to believe in hope even when it feels like it has let you down. Encouraging the children to dare to dream, to dust themselves off, to start again, to demand something more. From soon after the funeral service, the children began calling up towards the sky to Shay when they wanted him to know what mattered to them. It was their way to speak their truth. I'd encourage them to shout up their indignation that he wasn't there for their birthday or any disappointment. Gracie would whisper in my ear that she wanted her Daddy here like her friends had. She would beam as I passed her message on by shouting at the ceiling. We discovered that hope for us is an active word; it thrives on honesty, love and doing whatever it takes to shed feelings that weigh us down.

The summer after Brian and Grace had called up daily to Shay in the sky, they were out playing on the green in front of our house. They ran in, grabbing a hug from me.

"If Daddy was here he would play with us".

It happened that lots of their friends' Dads were out, kicking football, walking dogs. The children were miserable, lamenting how different their life would be if they only had their Daddy. I had to explain.

"Daddy only died love. There's a Chelsea football match on TV. If Daddy was here now he would be watching the game, there is no way that he'd be out on the green".

Often we put our dead on pedestals. The children need to grieve their real Dad. That way they can feel his real love. And Shay loved them so much.

CHAPTER 4

Shay

The best way to capture who Shay was in our lives is to look at the dignity that he brought to his own death. When Shay was eleven years old his father died. It was the typical experience of losing a parent back in the sixties. Almost nothing was said. Shay stood outside the closed door listening as his father groaned and vomited. The main clues to the seriousness of the situation were the hushed tones and pained look on his mother's face. Shay's mother was a gentlewoman. Petite, unassuming, a beautiful human being. Theirs was a house of few words. After weeks of listening at the door, Shay asked his mother "he won't die, will he?" She looked away in pain. Shay knew the worst. His next memory was the sombre funeral. Shay developed his own way to cope with grief by being exceptionally reliable, a 'good boy'.

Twenty years later, Shay woke up to himself when his first marriage ended in legal separation (divorce only became available in Ireland in 1997). Shay realised that when feelings get buried, they are buried alive. So he started a journey to uncover any hurt, to free up his feeling 'stuck' in the past, to be a better role model by becoming more assertive, to take responsibility for his own life.

A further driving force came from Shay's mother dying in 1992. Shay adored his Mum. He had vowed to himself to bring her on a special holiday. Shay's mum was such a quiet person, it felt like treasure to get her to admit a secret wish to visit Switzerland. Shay had tucked it away, waiting for his Mum to be freed from caring for an elderly aunt. His Mum died before the aunt. Afterwards, they discovered that his Mum had known for years she was dying but had wanted to protect them. This was Shay's first real encounter with what can feel like powerlessness in the face of cancer. As he grappled with the 'what ifs', Shay found himself drawn to stories of people who had survived against the odds. A common denominator was recognising and clearing blocks in your life, whether it is a room full of junk or an unresolved argument. That it is important to find the courage to face and release anything that brings stuck energy, fear or resentment.

For Shay the first step, after his Mum had died, was to do more to shed the silence of his childhood. To learn to say what was in his heart. This led him to increase his involvement with a support group (Beginning Experience) that he had found helpful when his first marriage had broken down. In time he became a facilitator. One of his most important lessons happened here. One weekend, I was dropping Shay off to facilitate a workshop for young people whose parents had separated or died (Young Adult Beginning Experience). As he entered the venue, he quickly turned to me and mouthed "I hope he's not in my group". Over Shay's shoulder I could see a young man in rainbow braces with a pageboy haircut, wonderfully camp. It happened that Shay had never knowingly met anyone gay before. His discomfort looked instinctual. Of course John was in Shay's group; they became wonderful friends.

Shay discovered that much of what he had believed all his life had belonged to someone else. His homophobia had no obvious origin. Yet, based on his reaction, he had learnt the lesson well. He had believed a version of life from the adults around him even though it wasn't his truth. Realising that he had little ownership of what he took for granted, it blew a hole in all his beliefs. He decided that the only way forward was to listen out for what was true for him in everything that he heard or thought.

So in 1999, when the medical team sombrely broke the news that he had a terminal form of cancer, Shay refused to be crushed by it. The very first words he spoke, when the team left the room having promised doom, was "Alan must not hear this from anyone else. The children will cope if they can trust every word out of our mouths. The truth is hard enough to deal with. I don't want them having unnecessary fears; I want to fight this."

Shay cared that friends and family should hear directly. Us naming it to everyone from the start helped him to break his tendency to silence.

Shay's courage was from the outset. His way to relate to what was happening was to imagine it through the children's eyes, to incorporate what he had learnt. He had felt guilty about the marriage break-up hurting Alan but he had presumed that he would be there to support him through it all. This new guilt, the possibility he would not be there for his kids, had the potential to drown him. Shay began listening to his body, learning to judge what he could cope with. Anything spare that he had, he wanted to keep to share with the children.

Before the diagnosis, Shay had had three weeks of exhaustive tests, This meant fasting almost every day so he had very little energy for the battle starting out. Facing the possibility of death head-on was liberating and terrifying all at once. We had heard that people who had beaten a prognosis had made this a priority, a first step. With each small victory we felt empowered. It was time to focus on the wisdom of changing what we could change, while letting go of whatever we had no control over. We committed to doing our very best, trusting that 'we would win'. For us, winning was whatever the outcome was; we couldn't do more than our best. It was such a hard road. We were stretched all the time.

We didn't have the power to stop Shay being physically taken from us. But, by working together, he wrapped us in an emotional blanket that buffered our first few years without him. Even now, whenever there is a special occasion, I organise a gift for the children from Shay. I sign it with a cartoon of Shay with wings. In the early days of diagnosis, Shay and I had spent a day window shopping, imagining what he might buy for the kids in anticipation of birthdays that he might miss. It was hard to do, but that means I don't feel quite so alone when I wrap their presents now. The practical gifts that have meant the most to them are the simple ones like their first cartridge pen. Their Dad being part of the moment means that he feels nearby all day in school.

Children are meant to leave home but Shay went first. There will come a point in time when they choose to change their connection to their Dad, probably when it shifts from being a warm cosy feeling to the idea of him watching over them seeming way too weird or embarrassing. In the meantime, they still feel the presence of their Dad... while Shay has the advantage that he gets to watch football all day now too.

CHAPTER 5

Secrets keep us sick

One of the greatest lessons of that time for me was how honesty brings joy. We had known this, but the diagnosis was a kick-in-the-pants reminder. It continues to be vital to the kids and my feeling good. As a widow, I notice couples who struggle to talk to each other, friends in pain. I find it difficult not to judge. I want to shake whichever partner is afraid to change. I'm jealous that they have the choice. Yet I also believe it is better to wake up beside an empty pillow than the wrong head. Only the people in a relationship know for sure if theirs is working or not. Our own truth is that it was in facing death we managed to fully 'show up' in the relationship. We did what felt like our best for years but the diagnosis put a bomb under us.

Suddenly there was no holding back. Both of us thrived on the feeling of coming home. Daring to be completely real was like finding the volume switch on fear and anxiety. Life felt softer, quieter in our hearts. We felt safe. For some reason we had always been wary of being totally real together. We prided ourselves on being honest but there were places that we had left untouched. Mainly those 'best not go there' places.

At one stage of crisis, Shay's homeopath suggested an exercise that delivered us to that place of 'home'. Shay was in shock having been told he was in renal failure. He sat vacant, broken. The renal failure had been avoidable, which made the despair deeper. I felt that I couldn't reach him. The exercise she offered was simple. I plonked a chair down in front of Shay and made him look at me. I was to reach deep inside and finish the sentence "I forgive you for…" until there was nothing left to say. I knew this might be the last conversation we ever had. I reached in to the unsaid moments of all the years to find the ones that still had a charge. Issues that I had forgotten were there. The silly places we lose each other as couples. The first one that came up that day was about farts.

Shay's mum used to serve high tea on a Saturday. Everything was delicious. One time, something in the food didn't suit my digestion. Unexpectedly, I let off a stinker. There was no escaping the odour. I was mortified. This was early days; I had wanted to make a good impression on his Mum. In my embarrassment, I looked to Shay for some understanding. He shot me a livid glare. I became a mixture of tearful and indignant. My way to deal with the hurt was to make sure I avoided ever letting off wind around him.

Twelve years later, sitting in the hospital room trying to reach this vacant Shay, I explained how I had unconsciously kept a baseline of squeezed buttocks for years. I still felt angry that he had somehow thought I'd done it on purpose that day. Shay stirred from the 'blown away' shock of the renal failure. As he listened to me it dawned on him that his reaction had been about the elderly aunt who had lived with them. She used to let off wind, belching and farting regularly and she had never apologised. Shay felt it was a terrible insult to his Mum who cared so well for this person. The look he shot in my direction was the pent up anger at this aunt, not me. If only we could have laughed together, naming it on the drive home that day. Instead, I used to plan road trips identifying loo breaks in advance in case a groan came out my rear end. So much energy wasted on a misunderstanding. Following that conversation, Shay had vivid dreams where lots of unanswered questions from his childhood fell into place. A weight of sadness lifted for him. What took us so long?

Giving the exercise a try, Shay forgave me for issues such as the way that I left kitchen cupboard doors open. It drove him nuts but he had given up mentioning it. I had made half-hearted attempts to keep them closed but it wasn't important to me, so I had never taken it seriously. Shay also voiced how difficult it was that I would discourage him from being angry. If I sensed that he was tense about something, I would cook his favourite food. If Shay was upset, I heard it as him being upset with me. I make my world safe by being a people pleaser. The problem is that when we avoid conflict, it doesn't go away; most of it ends up stuck inside the other person. It gets stuck in us too but we try to convince ourselves it has nothing to do with us. Shay knew that he had to find healthy ways to release the pent up anger of always having been a 'good boy'. I effectively kept telling him not to take it out around me. In my head there was something 'wrong' with anger; whereas now I get that what was wrong was the ways we had been taught to deal with it.

These were the moments that changed our lives together. Not

rocket science, just daring to look for the truth. We took turns to fill in the "I forgive you…" blanks until there was nothing left, except us grinning at each other. The colour was back in Shay's cheeks. Why did it take the fear that I might never get to talk to him again, to speak up about something as small as a fart? What did we miss by waiting until then?

Years before, pregnant, I found myself wondering how I had ended up with this man. As I was struggling in morning sickness, green with nausea, Shay would pointedly walk away. Bastard! One of the traits I loved about Shay was his kindness but this felt like a brute, especially in the excitement and trepidation of pregnancy. To be able to get out of bed in the morning I needed to eat a dry biscuit. I usually made sure I had some to hand, but sometimes I forgot. On the days with no cracker, I vomited as soon as I started moving. As I called to Shay for help, I would hear the front door slam. Chronic morning sickness meant that this wasn't an issue that could be ignored. When we eventually spoke, I was sobbing hysterically while he got quieter and quieter, hitting that place of clenched teeth resistance and indignation. We seemed to be at an impasse. To him I was being irrational, blaming him when he had enough responsibilities already. I sobbed in full hormonal flow.

"What would be so bad about getting me a cracker? What is the worst thing that could happen?"

Shay's resistance melted as it dawned on him why he was being so abrupt.

"You could die."

Shay realised that listening to his dad vomiting and then dying, had made him terrified of nausea in a loved one. Suddenly all the times he fussed about any of us drinking too quickly made sense. Or the times when he had tried to tell Alan to stop being carsick, as if a puking child had any control. Hormones had pushed us to talk. If we hadn't dared to be honest that day, we would have missed so much joy through the pregnancies. And Shay would have been left stewing alone in the worry of losing us. Daring to speak it out loud dissolved some of the power that it had to drag him down.

That's what I love about speaking our truth: the quality of release once we name what feels uncomfortable. Comedians thrive on it, shining lights on hidden aspects of our lives. When the audience erupts in laughter, some of the pleasure is the relief that comes with discovering we are the same as everyone else. Shay and I giggled at so much of life. It can seem a lot less funny without him now. When someone close to us dies, it is just 'shite'. What can we ever have faith in again? Where do we look to find it? The way forward seemed clear when Shay was here. Now I need to find a new map. The only ingredient that I am sure of is that I am committed to being honest. The next step is to figure out what is true for me so that I know what to be honest about.

CHAPTER 6

The diagnosis – what it meant for us as a family

As the consultant was explaining Multiple Myeloma, she mentioned that if the chemotherapy was successful we would be lucky to get three and a half years. Shay and I were clutching each other at the time.

I argued "But our new life is going to start then; we have plans to move to the country".

She responded. "Your life is now."

She was right.

Shay was clear that his priority was for the children to have a different experience than he'd had when his father was sick. Maybe he could make it so that their Daddy didn't die. Shay dedicated his energies to getting better. Our children can motivate us to move mountains, never mind climb them. From the outset, this was a family task. Grace was four months old. Some part of the pace of life felt like a continuation to the chaos of having a new baby. With the added flavour of living a nightmare from which we couldn't wake up.

Previously, while watching TV dramas, I had enjoyed spooking myself with the 'what if' of one of us having some horrible illness. Flirting with a fear made me appreciate what we often took for granted as a family. I had never believed it would actually happen; it was part of the entertainment of the drama. The fantasy had included our eyes locked in shocked silence as we digested the news, tinged with a hint of romance as appropriate music played in the background. It was never about talking in code over the children's heads or having to stop half way through a crucial piece of information to change a stinking nappy when fear already had my gut in turmoil.

Having been a health professional, I had more understanding of the different tests. Shay found it easier when I explained what might be going on. It was horrendous reading Mr Men books while continuing a conversation in disjointed half sentences, trying to reassure Shay and myself. We had thought that it might be coeliac disease and were naively happy when that was eliminated. When Shay was eventually diagnosed, he was still an in-patient. I was called in to speak with the doctor in the hospital. It seemed routine, Shay liked me to be there when they were explaining any results. I was breastfeeding Grace so she came too. A friend offered to drive and to mind Grace while Shay and I spoke to the consultant.

As the words of the diagnosis penetrated our ears, shock hit our bodies. We silently screamed 'no', trying to make the doctor stop talking. Within seconds, from down the corridor came a stereo howl from Grace. Afterwards, our friend said that it seemed to be completely unprompted. Any parents who have ever tried to make love with a breastfed child nearby, know how 'connected' they are. How they can sense our every nuance. So it was never a decision whether to include the children; we were in this together. Shay was fighting for his life, his family was his life.

Shay's honesty in the grief of the diagnosis guided us too. He dared to reach past guilt and fear, to choose to live. Shay had always been a people pleaser. It was hard for him to put himself first. Choosing to follow a programme of visualisation, special foods and treatments meant declining most visitors. It was equally hard for the visitors not to have easy access when they were worried sick about him. Shay held his own against the odds. He was pretty stable until a Hickman (a tube in the chest that had been left in unused for five months) caused septicaemia. The antibiotics required pushed him into renal failure. On dialysis, Shay was limited in the alternative approaches he could use. His best prognosis at this time was six weeks. The children witnessed the courage Shay brought to this shattering news. They were too young to understand about time, but they woke each morning sensing the joy in the air of every day we won past the six weeks deadline.

Shay lived a further fifteen months. The energy that made that possible was fuelled by facing the nightmare head on. On occasion, the children witnessed Shay cry, calling out in pain or in despair. It makes sense to a child that if you are hurting, you cry or scream. Why would you carry it around for the rest of your life? All that was happening felt like a bomb going off that sent ripples through all our lives. Shay understood that cancer was attacking his cells. For him, that was less of a threat than the way the cancer was attacking our dreams. The 'diagnosis' gave a medical name to what was happening in Shay's body. All the work he had done in recent years meant that he had moved from a place of depression to joy. Primary to his joy was his family. It felt like we were all being ripped from him. No bone pain came close to the agony of this. The only emotional pain relief available to Shay was to stay focused on the now, to value every nano-second.

When Shay had a short window of being able to read to the children, having them on hand meant that they got much more quality time. Au pairs, friends and family shared the load. My impulse as a Mum was to completely shield them from any of this, but we couldn't. It surprised us how well they coped. They seemed to feel safe in being able to trust our word. If there was something that needed worrying about, Mammy and Daddy would tell them. In the meantime, they just got on with it. Our task as parents was to keep vigilant to any pain being laid down at the time, to help them find ways to shed it. It still is.

CHAPTER 7

The diagnosis – what it meant in terms of the kids

Our first step was to release the kids from wanting to 'mind' us. Our baseline was that big people mind big people, big people mind little people, but little people never have to mind big people. This meant that the children would give us cuddles then run off to have fun. It made it easier for them to understand when we turned to friends for support; it helped them to trust that we were dealing with the yucky bits. It started as 'little people never mind big people' but the kids objected. They wanted to be part of the solution. So we adjusted it to 'never have to'. Being allowed to help in bite size pieces has taught them about compassion. Throughout, they could read us like a book, no matter how much we thought we had managed to hide it from them. They knew our blackest moments just by their breathing the same air as us. They sensed how much pain we were in even when we weren't paying attention to it ourselves. Children miss very little.

We discovered that the children often had different issues to what we assumed might be a problem for them. Grace was a year and three months old at the time of Shay's first admission to the hospice. We explained that Daddy was going away to get help to stop him vomiting. Grace was crestfallen. In her world, daddy's vomiting was entertainment. It was so dramatic, she was fascinated to see what came out of Daddy's mouth. Grace sulked whenever she heard the word 'hospice' for the first few days after Shay went in. Towards the end of his life, Shay occasionally used adult diapers. They were hideous blue monstrosities. The only positive that I saw was that maybe it would be nice for Grace that someone else in the house was in a nappy. The first time that Grace (then two years old) saw one on Shay, she stood wide-eyed for several moments. Then she stared at Brian who was five years old. From that moment she went dry. It was as if she thought "If I don't stop using these nappy things now, I will end up like that!" She shed hers on the spot, refused a replacement and never had an accident until months later, when she was grieving Shay.

Alan, being older, got to muck in with the practicalities. The hospice had suggested it was important that he got a chance to participate. As a teen, Alan had different needs to the small ones. Losing a parent in adolescence is more difficult than at any other time in life. The hospice team was brilliant at creating opportunities to help Alan and Shay to understand each other's needs. Teens have a sense of what loss can mean, at a time when they are just beginning to trust the potential of life. We desperately wanted it to not be happening, but it was. All we could do was try to make the best of what our lives had become.

Another heart-breaking factor for all of us was that children tend to blame themselves for anything that feels 'wrong' around them. With their limited understanding of the world, when a horrible feeling doesn't go away they presume they must be the problem. Most of their life experience has been that when they are faced with a collapsed sandcastle, either there is an identifiable sandcastle wrecker or it is their fault. If there is a yucky feeling with no obvious source, it must be something they unwittingly did themselves. When Shay was diagnosed, one of the ideas I used to describe to Brian as to what was happening was based on a freebie computer game we had recently got with a box of cereal.

Brian was four. Playing with the computer was still a new adventure. I tried to capture the magnitude of what was ahead of Shay. I explained that it was as if the doctor had handed Daddy a brand new computer game, with very few instructions, saying that Daddy needed to get to level ten straight away, that we had a big job on our hands. Life was chaotic with phone calls and hospital runs. Brian was very good pottering by himself. It took a while for me to realise that his quiet play was Brian dedicating himself to reaching level ten with the free cereal game, that he was trying to make everything right in our world. Telling children they are not to blame is not enough; they still feel the broken sandcastle feeling. Brian was distraught when I helped him to understand that his getting to level ten wouldn't make Daddy's cancer go away. Only Daddy could make himself better, no one else. Powerlessness in the face of a broken sandcastle feeling is even harder to swallow.

Not having had computers in our day, we discovered that games can be confusing in other ways too. Children learn that when someone dies, all you have to do is wait ten seconds for them to pop up again ready for whatever comes next. It can come as a surprise that there is no 'off' switch for death or grief. That it has to be experienced directly to be able to get to the next level.

We also learnt that children need clear signposts. We learnt this the hard way. Soon after the diagnosis, with the help of an artist friend, we had made a beautiful poster with the children. It said 'WE WILL WIN'. It took two years to realise that others saw this as total conviction on our part that Shay would live. It was so confusing for the children having people try to set them straight. It came from genuine caring but it missed the crucial element. We had explained that whatever came from doing our very best was 'winning'. The children needed it repeated regularly. I am one of those parents who talks too much at my kids even though I know that they need us to speak in short sentences with small words. In this case we said too little.

The children witnessed much of what was happening, which also meant that they had more opportunities to connect with Shay. I would lift Grace up to 'Daddy kiss' him by rubbing noses. Shay's smile breaking into complete bliss meant that Grace regularly saw how precious she was to her daddy. When we appreciate the very best of life, it is infectious. Shay was in a hospital bed downstairs for the last six months. The 'smallies' and I slept on a double mattress on the floor beside him. One night as Shay and I were settling down to rest, the children had been asleep a few hours already. There was a fire in the hearth. The flickering light danced across the walls and furniture. I topped up the fire with logs and replaced the fire screen in front it. Brian woke and came quietly to my side.

Replacing the screen changed the flickering. We noticed different shapes on the ceiling in the darkness. With the logs taking hold, the fire made the best light for shadow puppets. Brian and I put on a display for Shay. It was close to midnight. I've never been very good at making shadow puppets but something about this meant that the images were terrific. Our hushed giggles to avoid waking Grace added to the delight of it all. Brian had a book with pictures of how to make the shapes so he showed me to what to do. We ended up with mammy and baby versions, his little hands guiding with mine copying. For twenty minutes of rabbits, wolves, birds and aliens, Shay's joy glowed back at us. It had been a rough day but it ended with the lovely feeling of us plugged back in as a family.

CHAPTER 8

The diagnosis _ what it meant to dream

It might seem baffling that we appeared strong through this time. We were baffled ourselves. I would have sworn that you'd have had to scrape me off the floor. The medical teams commented that they had rarely met people so ready to face it all. But Shay had done the groundwork for years. He had wished that his mother had fought her cancer so that she might still be around. In his efforts to discern if this was reasonable, he had researched the basics of what can make the difference. He had a map of the territory.

A crucial element for us once Shay got over the shock, was that we worked as a team. Sharing the load. I mention this because for anyone going through a similar situation, it is not a team effort if one person does all the work. I have friends who have broken their hearts and their own bodies trying to do the work for their partner. It was Shay's fight; we were his allies. Shay filled his day with gentle exercise, vegan food, lots of juices, meditation, visualisation, homeopathy, osteopathy and getting rid of any clutter in his life or in his heart.

As I write, I personally know five people alive, kicking and cancer-free having been given terminal diagnoses. Two were diagnosed with advanced terminal cancer in the early 1990s. They are thriving, fitter than I am. They used a combination of approaches. Recovering and staying well takes commitment: choosing life on the basis that everything worth having costs. When Shay was sick we only knew one person, Shay's homeopath, who had beaten cancer using complementary methods. It helped, but Shay still doubted his own ability. Shay's openness to alternatives started when he decided that it had taken something 'weird' for him to get cancer, so it would probably take something 'weird' to get rid of it.

I've come to realise that it isn't so much about what one chooses to do, more the attitude behind it. Anyone I know who has defied a diagnosis recommends shedding feelings that keep us stuck, facing our fears. Shay and I discovered that when we faced our fears straight on, they were like paper dragons. Fierce and scary from a distance, but up close most of them held little substance. Being surrounded by people who have managed to place a question mark in front of a terminal diagnosis makes it a real possibility, giving hope in a tangible form.

There seem to be three fronts: physical, emotional and spiritual healing. These, woven together, give the best chance of a full recovery. What I have noticed in people who have been successful is that they give each equal attention. Usually one or two of the fronts seem to come a little easier depending on the person, but it's the balance of all three that seems to support a body back to health. It takes scrupulous honesty with a sense of adventure to take true ownership of our health. Health is more than staying alive. For me, this is key. We have a fear of dying that gets in the way of discovering what 'health' can be for each of us. Do we really want to work so hard to end up just existing? Being fully alive takes more. People who have defied their 'death sentences' grasp this. It radiates from them.

The last six months of Shay's life came from him realising that he had the power inside himself to change his life. When he seemed to be dying in February, something clicked that he had choice. It meant that he beat the odds again until August. Before finding his own power, his confidence had been grounded in the fact that others had managed it. He had read several success stories. Maybe, by holding on to their shirttails, he might get lucky too. A light switched on in his eyes the day he realised that it wasn't about luck; it was about the choices he was making from his gut. The power of his future was in his hands, in what he allowed to be a priority in his life. Instead of looking to someone else to have the answers, it dawned on Shay that living is about choice. Other peoples' stories gave him a map; he had to choose the way.

He wished he had had the tools to listen to his gut from the very start, as choices he had made early on seemed to be limiting his options now. Based on placebo theory, chemotherapy is more likely to work for people who believe in it. Shay didn't. But he also didn't take enough time to look at his options. At the time it seemed as though he had no other choices back in the shock of diagnosis. Recognising there was a strong chance he might die, he galvanised the energy to leave the hospice, to make sure that he was at home with his family if it was time to pass.

Choice is key. It is important that this doesn't translate into guilt. People can end up blaming themselves if it doesn't work out the way that everyone hoped. If we make a choice based on what feels light to us, it comes with an invitation not to judge the outcome. We are programmed to judge ourselves. People try so hard to beat cancer. It presumes we know the 'right' outcome. It's a bit like Grace 'telling' rather than 'asking'. If we believe there is something bigger than us when we ask, it's important that we realise we have done nothing 'wrong'. If the outcome is not what we hoped for. Shay did his absolute best to live. We can't do better than our best. We only have a small part of the overall picture. It's about living in the question because the truth is that no one can know for certain.

Here is a brief window into the difference it made for us to think outside the box and for Shay to take ownership of his life and death. We brought him home after seven months in the hospice, it was March. We were using a compound called 714x at the time. 714x works by detoxing the lymph system. It involves injecting the compound daily on a 21 day cycle. It took a little bit of getting used to but we soon relaxed. The homecare team were baffled as to how we were coping with such little analgesia. Initially, they seemed to suspect us of using some substitute opiate like heroin. The minimal doses of morphine taken by Shay made no sense to them. They would visit Shay, surprised to find him alert and comfortable.

Every day was a gift. We didn't appreciate how exceptional 714x was in terms of Shay's comfort in palliative care. We had seen a video of testimonials of people who had used this to cure themselves, including a doctor who had been diagnosed with ovarian cancer and was in remission against expectation. We wanted a cure. We decided to try a different approach, which meant coming off 714x first. We wanted to believe it was the medicine that lacked the vital ingredient rather than, by this stage, how Shay's body lacked the ability to find its way back. For 72 hours after changing from 714x, Shay was in unbearable bone pain with violent vomiting. This was what the hospice staff had been expecting all along. Eventually, the new approach kicked in. Here's a link to one of many stories of survivors:

http://www.youtube.com/watch?v=qUO4AzCMo7k

If you want to know more check out:

http://www.cerbe.com

There is an advice line to answer questions. We found them extremely helpful and honest.

The only reason we were able to try the different approaches was because Shay's workmates had mega-fundraised. They were and still are amazing in their friendship and support. It's possible to waste a pot of money on internet promises of cures for cancer. By the same token, there were products that made a significant difference for us that are also listed as rubbish in Quackwatch. This wasn't our experience. The hospice and dialysis teams were very involved. They conceded that the differences we were witnessing could not easily be dismissed as placebo. For example,

Shay's creatinine (a measure of kidney function) decreased from having been 850mmol/L-1000mmol/L for twelve months to 350mmol/L, with no medical reason for this reversal. It didn't even make sense in medical terms that he had lived the twelve months before it started to reduce. There was no medical explanation for it coming down to 350mmol/L. We had great advice. It's important to do good homework before spending any money. The desperate hunger to find a cure makes all of us vulnerable to charlatans.

Buyer beware.

CHAPTER 9

The diagnosis _ what it meant on the medical side

Medicine uses statistical evidence to guide treatment. The moment that Shay decided to step outside the box of expectation, he stopped qualifying as a statistic. This posed a problem in our communication with the doctors; their predictions didn't automatically apply to Shay. Research does not allow for individuals taking a different approach. We would have loved to share, to ask, to explore. Mostly we nodded and said nothing. Some staff whispered their encouragement.

"Shay, keep doing whatever you are doing because you are looking great." Inherent in the lowered voice was a message to keep this covert.

Shay was pleasantly surprised whenever staff responded positively, supporting him to take ownership of his health. We could feel their respect. This helped him to feel confidence in their word when exploring options. Shay and I had no desire to reject western medicine. We welcomed any possibility that increased Shay's chances to stay. Why does it become an issue of all or nothing, rather than the best of both approaches? It's about listening to our bodies, not anyone else. For example, the safest place for a mum to choose to have her baby is the place where she feels safest. For me that was at home. For lots of friends that was hospital. I was deeply grateful to know that if my babies or I needed it, there was a hospital nearby. It happened that we didn't need it; nature did a wonderful job. But the amazing technology that exists today has kept many precious babies alive. Anyone being purist about one approach risks denying life.

The majority of staff were great. Some were exceptional. We felt their caring, their friendship. When the septicaemia struck, one gem who had been on the ward at the time of Shay's diagnosis happened to be passing as he was being re-admitted. When he heard what had happened, he put his head around the door and chirped "He'd be safer in a chip shop." We cracked up, laughing and crying. At random times his head would appear around the door with his one-liner that said everything. "He'd be safer in a chip shop."

Occasionally there would be a member of staff who didn't seem to meet us or our needs. At first, it was difficult to reconcile. We didn't have time to waste on their being poor at their job, or on us being angry at their limitations. It eventually occurred to us that the only way they would understand our urgency was if they were facing the same mountain as us. We wouldn't wish this on anyone, so we released our expectations of them. We wished them well in what felt like their blissful ignorance. Shay and I were all too aware of our version of being human, our less than perfect bits. Shay figured that some unresolved hurt from his childhood was showing in cancer. Maybe some of their hurt was showing by not being able to be fully present doing their job.

Sometimes, they inadvertently helped. In 1997, Shay had experienced extreme rib pain. X-rays were taken that came back clear. Once Myeloma was identified in 1999, the old x-rays were reviewed. 'Multiple fractures with swiss cheesing' was identified on the films that earlier had been declared 'no apparent disease'. These are classic signs of Multiple Myeloma. I felt twisted with indignation, distraught at all of the unnecessary pain that Shay had suffered. Whereas Shay's immediate response was "we would never have had Grace if we had known. Grace is joy. I wouldn't have wanted to know, if it meant not having her".

Shay placed a request on his chart that entitled me to be included in all treatment decisions. There were times that a doctor couldn't have looked more surprised at either my or Shay's contribution than if the bed itself had spoken. It tended to be the first time that they met us. They seemed unused to patients and families taking initiatives. Being open seemed to correlate directly with a measure of the Doctors' confidence in their own ability. Some celebrated Shay for taking ownership of his life; others seemed to want to slap us like errant children.

Except for declining further chemo, Shay was a compliant patient. We were a little unorthodox; we started by getting clearance to bring a small fridge into his room. We bought a new one so it was straightforward for the hospital's engineering department to approve it. This meant that I was able to bring freshly made nut-milks and juices. Shay found these gave him more energy than hospital food.

Some staff went out of their way to help. Right down to the little old ladies who pushed the drinks trolley around the hospice. Once a week they appeared with a full range of favourite tipples, creating a party atmosphere for patients and close carers. I usually declined as I would need to drive back to the house soon. One day, when I knew I was staying, I asked for a Baileys with ice. It warmed my frazzled body. A week later, in the early hours of the morning after Shay had been unwell, I discovered a glass of Baileys they had left for me on their rounds the day before. Each week after that, there would be a Baileys covered in the fridge. It mattered so much that they remembered me, to feel that visible. Their kindness always felt like a warm hug.

Our needs were inevitably greater than can be met in a hospital. One night I was torn leaving Shay. I was needed at home for the children but I ached to stay with him. Shay wanted me to stay too. It was agony to walk away. I met one of the night nurses on my way out. I passed on some practical messages and wished her a good night. She sighed, bemoaning the prospect of the night ahead of her. I knew it was irrational, but I wanted to explode. She should appreciate that she was getting to be in Shay's company for the night. She was getting what I wanted more than anything. I grudgingly understood why the privilege was lost on her. The nurse probably had her own whole world of wanting to be somewhere else. She was only being paid to care for Shay, not to love him the way we did. I walked away still wanting to shake her for not appreciating how lucky she was.

Shay wasn't up to visitors but he needed their support. At the start, with each round of chemo I would text his workmates, family and friends. They were brilliant at sending in fresh cards to cheer him up. We covered the walls of his room with the cards and drawings from all the kids. It changed the atmosphere. Getting so much post on the ward seemed to change the staff attitudes to Shay too. It helped to remind them that he had another life, that Shay was more than his diagnosis.

When he had beaten a number of 'die by dates', younger doctors voiced their support by inviting us to feel free to say what would help.

"You'd be dead by now if it had been left up to the system; let us know what you need."

They couldn't give Shay his life back but by seeing him as more than a number they gave him dignity. They were terrific practical support. We met some of the best nurses on the planet too. Thank you, to each of you.

After one particular crisis, I was pushing Grace in the buggy down a hospital corridor with Brian holding on to the side. We were chatting about Brian's school that day. It was a long and busy corridor. One of the doctors, who had admitted Shay the night before, appeared beside us. He gently knelt in front of the buggy. There was a passion about him as he looked the children in their eyes and said "Don't you ever doubt how much your Daddy wants to be here with you. I have never seen a man fight so hard to be with his family."

The children beamed back at him in pride that this was their Daddy he was talking about. This doctor man was saying that their Daddy was the bestest.

The dynamic between us and the medical team reminds me of any authority figures at times when we want to change our lives. Those people who seem to have power over our happiness, whether it is the boss, our friends, families, doctors, church, or people on our street. It's less about them and more about the degree to which we give our power to them. If we are trying to battle an addiction, walk away from an abusive relationship or a horrible job, choose health, follow a dream… we need to figure out our relationship with the people who we perceive as having power before we can make the best choices for ourselves. To change what we can. Shay's challenge was whether he could change enough to live. Having always been a 'good boy', it was daunting to step into his potency. It felt like he was standing up to the medics. He needed them on his side, pissing them off didn't seem very clever. It was a huge stress for him. What swung it for him was the suggestion "Treatment needs to be your choice. It is much easier to live with any consequences if you are clear that you were the one who made the choice."

From the outset, Shay's response was "Someone somewhere knows how to beat this but we may not find out in time." Shay's cancer was Multiple Myeloma. Soon after he died, a self-help book was released by a man in Oxford who also had Myeloma. He was in remission, against all odds. It's rare and special when someone beats a terminal diagnosis but it is possible. Sadly it wasn't for us.

CHAPTER 10

Being human

There were many times that we got it completely wrong. There is nothing neat about a diagnosis of terminal illness. Not at any stage. Both Shay and I made mistakes all along the way. It matters to me to share how human we were. I realise that the missing ingredient for me in 'made it through' stories is angst. By the time people arrive where they want to be, they appear to have shed much of their personal angst before they write the book. But my bucket-load of angst is the reason I picked the book up looking for answers. I find myself searching for subtext of the person's messy bits. Not to drag them down to my level but in the hope that maybe there is a chance I can get up to theirs. Otherwise, I simply get to admire their success, like watching people who climb Mount Everest, or sail around the world. I am in awe, but pretty confident that it won't be happening to me any time soon. Every change in life brings some angst. This means that they must have had some. Mine can be pretty intense so I need something hard core to get me through. I need to be confident that their journey might translate into mine.

In Shay's search to find ways to beat cancer, we came across 'The Journey' by Brandon Bay, who had found a way to heal herself. A 'Journey for Kids' was developed from her approach; a fun way to access and release deeply stored pain for young people. This approach has been adopted in state schools in South Africa to help the country heal from apartheid. When Grace was five and Brian was eight years old, I heard of an excellent facilitator who had organised a day of the process. Driving home after the session, happy that I had made it happen, I listened to their stories. It's a great process. I hoped that it might bring them some peace.

As we drove away, Grace proudly showed me a drawing she had done. It was a face that I could only glimpse at while I was steering the car, but it left quite an impression. She explained "They said to draw a picture of angry."

Grace was five at the time; I was stunned at how expressive her picture was. The face was ugly and contorted. As I was digesting this, she continued

"They told me to draw a picture of angry, so I drew you Mammy."

The shock that hit me was a mixture of deep pain, indignation and guilt. I had thought that I was managing to contain my rage at life. Grace clearly wasn't fooled.

Three years before, as the colder weather descended after Shay's death, I had moved the sand pit inside to the playroom because playing with sand seemed to help the kids. One morning, in exhaustion, I had fallen back asleep. The children, unsupervised, emptied the entire sandpit down the hall. I woke to find what looked like a 'board walk' right up to the front door. I exploded.

I remember Brian's eyes were like a rabbit caught in headlights. He had never seen me this furious.

Grace explained "That's a picture of the day you were cross about the sand in the hall Mammy."

In the rear view mirror I could see Brian watching cautiously, checking my reaction as Grace was filling in the details. This was three years post sand event, my explosion had left scars. My memory of the sand-covered hall was feeling sorry for myself having to clean up the mess. At the time I had registered their shocked little faces, but this had seemed a basic requirement to deter them from doing something like this again.

I apologised. We talked about what had happened back on the sand day. Brian explained that he was trying to see how far he could last running with a sieve full of sand down the hall. He had been chuffed that he had made it to the front door after several attempts. They then perfected the method, using the remains of about eight kilos of sand in the pit. I woke to a boardwalk in my hall. We love the beach so Brian had thought I would be happy. My eruption had come as a complete surprise to him. I suppress anger most of the time. This had been a pressure cooker erupting, with the kids getting the full force.

So we made a point of spending time together doing things that helped to get the residual anger out, without hurting each other. Lots of streams and rivers with throwing stones were involved. We would return home feeling a bit better. Then it would dawn that I had done nothing to organise food. Take-away again. We got to know the staff in the chip shop particularly well the first six months after Shay had died. I seemed to manage little more than one task a day. If that didn't include preparation of a meal, then it was thanks to the take-away that my kids got fed. Even three years later when I was 'landed', I had managed to forget to include food in the equation when we started dealing with feelings.

Snippets and anecdotes can paint a rosier picture than actually existed. There is no easy or superhero way of doing cancer or parenting alone. When I brought the children to buy new shoes after Shay died, they both had grown two sizes bigger since the last time they were measured. We had never noticed. Their need was under our noses but we were too busy with the drama of all of our lives to pay attention. This book started out with me saying that I want change. That starts by dealing with what is. I want to connect with people who recognise the struggle, not a tidy version.

Shay and I were both ourselves. The challenges helped us to see strengths that we hadn't known were there, but our baseline was the same. All we had was 'us' to apply to what was coming in our direction. Crisis tends to bring out our chronic behaviours. From an onlooker's point of view, I appeared to meet any of the challenges thrown at us. Made juices, sourced and measured concoctions, remembered to pay the mortgage, buy nappies. I drove back and forth to support Shay and the kids. In the quiet and peace of the car, I got closer to what I was really feeling. I was overwhelmed by my helplessness. My family were in pain, I couldn't make it right. That fed an internal rage, alongside what seemed like unending demands. So I did what was familiar, I stuffed my fears back down by eating. Some of it was medicating myself with food so as to get through the next hour. I was exhausted, food helped to keep me awake. My quick fixes tended to be fast-food and chocolate based, rather than organic, sprouted and wholesome.

One of my deepest doubts that we would 'pull it off' for Shay was because I was avoiding my real feelings. Allowing the drama of our lives to drown out the 'why me, why us?' that was raging in my gut. A major way that I managed was by being addicted to chaos. The buzz of permanent stress meant that I felt alive in a warped way. It distracted me from what lay deep inside, a screaming at the hell we had woken up in. Our plan had always been to grow old together. Our dream was slipping through our hands like water. We are as healthy and unhealthy as the person we are with. I knew that total remission for Shay was unlikely to work if I was less than well. No matter how clean skinned and bright eyed Shay looked, I was permanently stretched, aching, tired of running after our lives.

Without it being an equal journey, balanced and supportive of us both, there was a good chance we were missing the fundamental element needed to make a miracle happen. My default is to put all my energy into rescuing people. Put me in a room of ten people and within moments I could tell you what all nine others of them might need. Yet I can struggle to know what I need. I got lost in Shay and the kids needing me. Then, we lost Shay. If we don't find a way to shift, our oldest habits can be the undoing of our biggest dreams.

At one stage, feeling like a mess, I asked Shay to ask me how I was. People automatically asked how Shay was. I knew their concern included us. This day, I realised that months had passed since someone had directly asked me how I was. I needed to hear myself speak what was going on for me too. It really helped that Shay made a point each day after that of asking how I was and what was going on for the kids. Previously, I had confided in Anne that I felt like a bit of a cow for begrudging the attention on Shay.

"I know his life is precious, I really do."

Anne replied "Of course it is, but your lives are precious too."

I expect that carers reading this will get what I am trying to say. It was one thing to commit to living in the 'now'. It was harder to stay upbeat about living in the moment when all of life's focus had become a to-do list, with very few to-dos that had anything to do with me. I felt like I was becoming invisible to myself. I suspect that I would have cracked under the pressure if we hadn't been in it together, feeling seen by Shay when I was so tired that I barely knew I was there. I am not sure how carers who spend years in 100% giving-mode cope.

There were two of us doing our own particular tangos of sabotaging in terms of Shay beating the cancer. When Grace was on the way, we were a household of a fifteen year old, a three year old, Shay with undiagnosed cancer and a pregnant me. Mixing toddlers and teens in the same house can be a challenge. We opted for a service called teen counselling. We arrived to the first appointment trying to look the sort of 'normal' families aspire to look for school events. John (not his real name) met us at the door. A good lad who put us at our ease, John launched into suggesting that most people who come to a service like this have a story. Eventually, having shared it, they come to a point of action. They change.

John offered "How about we go straight to that point?"

A little baffled, we nodded.

"Who does the dishes?"

Shay and Alan muttered "whoever cooks doesn't do the dishes."

"So who cooks?"

Shuffling feet, the lads replied "Miriam."

"Who washes the dishes?"

"Miriam most of the time."

John turned to me, asking me to describe what happens. I explained how Alan tended to slip away at the end of the meal.

"What do you do about that?"

"I say, 'Alan what's the story?'"

"Stop right there. That implies dialogue. A teen will never want to do dishes. The most you say is 'Dishes. Do them, now'. Your homework is to go home and whoever cooks doesn't do the dishes."

I wished that I could have recorded him for so many mums I knew. A fortnight later we returned. John looked to Shay and Alan.

"Well, did you do the dishes?"

Alan proudly replied "I did my share."

Shay clearly hadn't the same confidence.

"Shay, why do you think that you avoid dishes?"

"Miriam says it's probably because my mother did everything for us, but I'm not sure".

In soothing tones, John offered "Shay, could I make a constructive suggestion?" Shay melted in relief that here was a kindred spirit. Nodding, he looked to John.

John bellowed "Get over it, the dishes need doing. Go home and do the dishes." Once Shay recovered, we chuckled all day. He changed for a while but then slipped into old habits. For some reason he detested doing the dishes. He did the laundry, ironing and bathroom, but avoided the dishes at every chance.

A few years later, Shay was bed bound due to the Myeloma. On a day when I had been up for over fifteen hours already, I went to organise the evening meal for all of us only to discover that there were no clean dishes. In despair, I filled the dishwasher twice. Eventually, I returned to Shay and the children with some grub. As we were eating supper, I kept yawning every time I opened my mouth for the next forkful.

"Shay, you beat this cancer and the dishwasher is yours for six months, love."

It took few moments for me to notice the look of total consternation on Shay's face. I was clear that I had earned any break. Shay continued to look fraught at the prospect of that many loadings and un-loadings. It slowly dawned on me.

"You might give up. You might die just to avoid doing the dishes."

Peevishly he conceded that it was a possibility. This man had defied science against the odds but it seemed washing up was a challenge too far.

CHAPTER 11

How close by is he?

On one of the times that Shay did 'a Lazarus', every symptom implied that this was the end. Shay looked shattered but was holding on. I asked him if he was afraid of what lay ahead. I tried to reassure him that we would be fine, that I believed he would end up in a good place. Shay was frail, struggling to breathe, his eyes crinkled as he replied "I just don't want to miss a second with you and the kids." By the next day he had baffled the medics again, he was back with us. If Shay could create this when he was a mere mortal, surely he would find a way to reach us from the other side.

Shay had great dress sense. I would urge him that he had to live because the kids needed him to help pick out their outfits for Communion and Confirmation. If the balance isn't right, it can look completely naff. I knew I had the potential to hit 'naff'. Shay talked me through the ideas he had always had of what they might wear. Brian made his Communion three years after Shay died. I brought him to Arnott's department store, where most of us had been fitted as children. I found the jacket and the trousers that Shay had described, but I couldn't find the exact shirt. I asked the sales assistant. She shook her head dismissively. "We haven't had those in ages. They will be snapped up as soon as they come back in."

It wasn't possible to pre-order. I was pretty frantic. Shirts mattered to Shay. It felt deeply important to honour his wishes. As I was leaving the children's department, I passed a rail with the right type of shirt. I brought the shirt to the sales assistant, apologising for not having been clearer.

"It was one like this that I meant. Where are these, please?"

She stared in amazement. "I haven't seen one of those for at least six weeks."

I pleaded "but I need one like this in his size."

She nodded towards Brian. "That is his size".

She took the shirt to wrap, all the time muttering "you were meant to have this shirt. You were definitely meant to have this shirt."

Brian and I looked at each other sideways. We said nothing while she kept commenting on how mad it was, how we must have been meant to have the shirt. This was pretty amazing so I was surprised that Brian and I weren't more elated. I felt fussed and confused.

Outside, it dawned on me. Three years of missing Shay, along with the fact that I was heading home to a broken dishwasher and a huge pile of dishes. If he could organise a shirt, where the hell was he when I needed help in the kitchen? Or when I ached for him to hold me at the end of an exhausting day? The next day, I was telling Anne on the phone. She burst out laughing, reminding me "Mir, he only died love. He didn't change. Would he have cared about the shirt for the child? Yep. Would you have had to nag him about fixing the dishwasher? Yep too, girl!"

I had forgotten that he only died.

Shay and I had spoken at length about what it might be like if he died. What would stop him from reaching me? I asked him to be really clear in any messages. I wasn't into looking at birds in formation and wondering if it was a sign from him. Shay died on a Thursday night. On Saturday morning there was a lull of visitors for the Wake. It allowed me time for the preparations. The house was empty except for me, the kids, and Shay's body. Friends phoned to check how we were. They were concerned that I was on my own. I found myself repeating "Thanks. See you later. We are really fine. Shay is still here."

Shay's funeral was so unorthodox that it meant much of the organising fell to me. I had just ordered two hundred helium balloons for the 'last birthday party' when my mobile rang. 'Shay mobile' appeared on the flashing screen. I bolted to go to him. Towards his death, I had only ever left him to go to the loo. He in turn only phoned me if it was something very urgent. As I flew down the stairs, it dawned on me: this call couldn't be Shay. It must be the kids messing with the phone. I was relieved that it meant that Shay wasn't in distress. I continued down to where I had left Shay's phone charging beside the coffin (I had needed contacts from his address book for the funeral). My phone was still ringing, flashing 'Shay mobile'. The phone plugged in beside him was flashing 'Mir Mobile'. The children were engrossed watching a cartoon in a different room, quite a distance away. I stood beside the coffin laughing. "Nice one, Shay." Afterwards, I contacted the mobile phone company to ask was there any interference that could have caused the phone to ring mine. They said no.

The first time I realised that Shay is still a vital part of all our lives was when I was driving away after leaving the children for a sleepover. Grieving children tend to feel the cold more and Brian had become dependent on his hot water bottle for sleep. Understandably, since it was summer, the sleepover parents didn't see the relevance. There wasn't time to explain. Brian's face was forlorn. He would have been fine if I had known to prepare him. I also knew that he would hate it if I made a fuss. As I drove away, I found myself screaming up towards the heavens. "Shay get your butt over there now, the kids need you".

Howling at the moon was a healthy release for me, like the way the children had loved to call up to Shay when they wanted him to know something. In my own anger at his death I had only shouted at him in my head. It felt like we expected a response by speaking it out loud. As I drove on I wished that, like the kids, I believed this was a dialogue. The grown up in me registered the silent void of the night sky. Just then, a doe jumped out of the ditch straight across the bonnet of the car. I missed her by an inch. The reflection in her beautiful brown eyes and shining fur that I glimpsed was fragile and magnificent. I was reminded that there is more to life and death than we will ever understand. I laughed up at the sky and said "thanks pal, I needed that. Now get over to the kids!"

This possibly sounds a bit lame to people who haven't felt what I am trying to capture. The incident was that a deer jumped across my path when my attention was elsewhere. Yet instead of being startled, something filled my heart at that moment that exploded in joy and peace. I was in awe of nature. I was reminded as I drove along that what I perceive as the 'reality' of our lives is such a small taste of what is available to us.

Since Shay died we have had many lovely moments that feel more than coincidence. I know in my heart that he is not far away. It took a long time for me to be able to trust it though. Mainly out of the pain of wanting him here in the flesh. The moment the possibility of him being around surfaced, there was a toddler tantrum inside that arose, wanting him here, now, 100%.

I had always presumed that feeling connected to loved ones was based in a need on the part of those left behind, a way to cope with the void left by death. I didn't mind the idea of being deluded if it diluted the pain. Years ago, I heard a theory that suggested it was necessary to stop pretending they are near so as to really let go when dealing with grief. I do think I have had authentic 'let go' moments, but I am convinced that he has been near too. I recognise the Shay that I sense there. It feels more than filling the yearning ache to see him. It feels like coming home. Staying in denial, if that is what it is, will not help us to heal. Yet to suggest that there is nothing there, that Shay is now simply his ashes, doesn't fit for us.

Sometimes it is as straightforward as it helps the excruciating rawness of grief, to imagine our loved ones are still in our lives. Back when Shay was diagnosed, I was often stuck at home with the 'smallies'. Alone in the hospital, Shay would concentrate on doing a meditation or visualisation. My only way to feel close to him was to do the same at home to support him. Shay would phone to say that he was starting. I would sit with the children, Grace feeding or asleep in my arms. Brian would cuddle up beside me and we would send golden light to Daddy. We did this almost every day, usually lasting about twenty minutes our end. Almost as soon as Grace could talk she would insist "pwink" for the light she would send DaDa.

A few weeks after Shay died, we were on a beach playing all day. As the sun was setting, Brian looked up to the horizon.

"Gracie, Gracie, look, Daddy is sending you back pink light".

The pink hues that filled the sky had a foundation of gold. Every sunset since has held us in a hug from Shay.

CHAPTER 12

Single surviving

If writing this is an effort to show you what you might not see sitting beside me on a bus, then I want to explain what it means to parent on my own. Chances are there is plenty that shows on the outside declaring in neon lights – single parent. Frazzled hair, mismatched socks, a fraught look. There is an inner experience of parenting on my 'tod' which is a bigger deal than I expected. My black and white of marriage was that we would live happily ever after. Waking up single feels like I'm being punished for something but I'm not sure what I've done. Being a widow I get to wear my rings. I find that this makes a difference. It is more socially acceptable to say that my husband left me by way of a coffin. I am not sure how this makes me any 'better' than friends who had the courage to face the sham of their relationship or when one parent simply walked out the door. The reality is that he still went, the needs are the same but the experience can be different. All parents need support. Single parents need a bit extra.

Shay died the week starting the autumn term at school. Brian wanted to return to school the day of the funeral. He settled for going in two days later. Having had to hand Brian over to a friend to bring to school for the previous year, it was lovely to have the time to walk to school together; Grace in the buggy, with Brian full of chat. A few days in, two envelopes were given to me by one of the teachers. Always having been in trouble in school myself, I felt like I was opening a school report. Inside were sympathy cards. Sobbing at their kindness, I hurried home. Through the blur of tears I read "You know that we love him and that we will mind him". I sat nursing the cards, rocking back and forth. I had spent months with my antennae out trying to cover every eventuality, feeling so inadequate. In my grief, it seemed as though Shay having died was proof of my inadequacy. Now I was all the children had. The teachers were saying that I could exhale about Brian, they had my back. He would be safe and held at school.

Later that day, I was in touch with a friend in another town. Her daughter is the same age as Brian and her younger child has autism. The Dad had walked out that week. The only way that the mum could manage the full-time care of her children was to pay someone to stay in the house at night when the kids were asleep. She worked a nightshift in a factory. Then, with little or no rest, she managed the additional needs of her child through the day. She hadn't yet had a chance to talk to her daughter's teacher. When I urged her to, she was self-conscious about the stigma of separation. What if the teacher didn't approve? It might mean the teacher would treat her little girl differently (divorce had only been made legal in Ireland four years earlier). Something is seriously wrong with this picture. Brian's teachers can never fully know what their cards meant to me in terms of shared parenting and kindness. Whatever opinions one has about any adult choices, it takes a village to bring up children. Our children need more from the village sometimes.

Another gift that meant the world was from a neighbour who knocked on the door Christmas week, the year Shay died. Quiet and gentle, she presented a beautifully wrapped parcel. Most people had arrived with two presents. I wondered what she had brought for the kids that came in one. I hoped that it wouldn't lead to wars between them. It was prettily wrapped. Geraldine placed the gift in my hands.

"That's a little something for you. I figured you might be missing a main present under the tree this year; I wanted you to have something nice."

Christmas morning, as the children ripped into the wrapping papers, I opened my gift. It was a beautiful blouse that fitted perfectly. Geraldine is now a cherished friend. Back then she was a neighbour with a huge heart.

Being single means a quality of loneliness where any gentleness brings deep pleasure. It nurtures a hope that life can have softer edges again. Shay and I had always cared about single parent friends. A few years earlier, a friend had commented that we seemed to understand more than anyone else what it was like for her. We thought we did, but we hadn't a clue. It came as a surprise to me how hard being a single parent can be. Every bill, every light bulb, every decision, the plumbing, the fuse box, what school to pick, every blade of grass... is my responsibility.

Actually, I did have help with the blades of grass. The only reason my house didn't look like a squat was because our next door neighbours were like garden elves. This couple made our garden sing. It was their way to support us when Shay was sick. He was so grateful. They created a beautiful space for him to spend time with the children. When Shay died, I knew my priority was that the children needed home to be a haven, a place where they could recover from the world. Pat and Jacqui, the garden elves, helped to make this possible. In time, the garden's care reverted to me. It became functional rather than pretty but at the crucial time when the children needed to recover from shock, it was a place of beauty where they played happily for hours.

As I write, I am aware that lots of single parents I know would read this and immediately think "She's right. The garden needs to be nicer for the kids". The to-do list is unending for any parent but there is a further quality in a single parent's life. In fact, single parenting is a contradiction for me. I can't single 'parent'. I find that it's all I can do to single 'survive'. I want to do my very best, but my best back then was that the kids were lucky that I managed to keep a roof over their heads and to feed them the year after Shay died. Having to leave a sick child alone in the middle of the night, while searching for the thermometer, is heart-breaking. So many parents know this feeling. Eventually, with each new difficult moment, I organised our lives differently, like moving supplies upstairs to hand. I always felt that I was falling short of what needed to be done. I still feel less than what is needed but I don't give myself the same hard time about it now.

Not knowing what to do is another factor. The lights 'blew' in our spare room a few years ago. I changed the bulbs, but still no joy. Without Shay to consult, we started using a torch to get to the lamp in the room by the bed. I felt chuffed at how inventive I had become, finding ways to cope. I remember being organised by making sure I had spare batteries when a guest was coming to stay. It was only when they looked at me with incredulity that I expected them to use a torch, that it dawned on me this may not be everyone's way of managing. It felt good that I could find the torch and figured that I was touching on 'super mum' having back-up batteries. They seemed bemused rather than impressed.

I could have asked for help. Not asking is partly because I am more comfortable giving rather than receiving. But my main motivation has been to save up others' goodwill for when I really need it. The world seems bigger and more fraught on my own. Shay's diagnosis caused havoc in our lives but there were two of us. What if another 'bomb' went off with just me?

One time when we were in a restaurant, Brian wanted salt for his chips. He was eight years old. I told him to go across the room to ask a waiter. A nearby diner shot me an indignant look that said that I was an uncaring and irresponsible mother. Brian was nervous of asking. I put more energy into cajoling him to do it than would have taken to get it for him myself. The nearby diner was clearly irate. One parent with two kids means that the only way of managing in a crisis is that the children learn some autonomy. I was a mum practising when it didn't matter, to give Brian better coping strategies because there was a chance he might need them some time we were in a crisis. At any moment he could find himself 'in charge' without the luxury of the other parent arriving on the scene to take over and make it better.

Perhaps it was due to an issue from this other diner's childhood that they were triggered by us, some time when they felt unheard and unsupported by their own parents. I had enough on my plate. I didn't need their stuff too, especially since it was clear that, in their eyes, there was only one person with any issues that needed addressing. That would be me.

CHAPTER 13

Shay-less

A week after the funeral I needed to make an urgent visit to the bank as lots of our life had gone untended towards the end. There were five comfortable seats against the wall and a narrow, not very child-friendly, queue. The doors were locked so I was pretty confident Grace couldn't escape. I got the children to pick a chair each to sit in so they could pass the time by looking at their books. I asked them to wait patiently, with promises that I wouldn't be long and a treat afterwards for being good. Just as my place in the queue meant that I got to the desk, I heard a hideous racket of children squabbling. My first impulse was a self-righteous "That's dreadful. My children would never behave that way." I began to deal with the cashier. The noise became untenable so I turned around in indignation. I didn't want my children witnessing this type of behaviour. Of course it was my two causing the riot, fighting like cats and dogs over one of the chairs. I had to complete the transaction. Waiting for the lady to stamp and sort, I called to the children to behave. They paid no heed. It served me right for having been so quick to judge earlier. I looked sheepishly at the queue behind me, seeking a shared parent smile. Embarrassed, I hoped for some quality of acceptance or support. Each person in the queue averted their eyes from mine. We were untouchables.

Puce with humiliation, I couldn't risk anything other than dragging them to the car. Later, I asked them what had happened. I needed to understand what it was about the chair that they both had to have it. Brian said that Grace always got the best things. All five chairs were identical. Eventually Brian added that Grace got to see Daddy more when he was sick. As I began to explain to Brian that he was right, that Grace had been at the hospital and in the hospice more than him, Grace interrupted in fury. She struggled to find words in her two year old indignation. In her memory of events, Brian was the one who always got to go to Shay. There had been one evening when Brian had been brought to us in the hospice by a friend of Shay's. Grace had been made stay at home with my mum. This was what had imprinted on Grace; watching Brian being driven away while she wriggled in Nanny's arms. In her world that meant that she had always had the shorter straw.

Grace being a toddler was a liability in Shay's hospice room. Her favourite occupation was to clean his en-suite loo with his toothbrush. I gave in and bought several to cover the times that we forgot to make sure it was out of harm's way. The bathroom was wheelchair accessible; Grace was tall so with a bit of ingenuity she could reach everything. The evening of Grace staying home with Nanny, we had wanted to play with Brian in a chilled atmosphere. A change from the constant interventions of trying to ensure the hospice was intact after the kids' visit. Despite explaining this as much as possible to Grace, she remained convinced that she had had the rougher deal. Brian then felt even 'harder' done by. It became a really big issue who got to sit directly beside me in any situation. When it was at a table, I could never get through to them that the one sitting across from me was actually getting more attention as they were in my direct sight. Being a single parent can feel like always being less than enough.

It was never meant to be this way. The dolls we played with as kids never came with divorce papers. I never dressed Barbie in a widow's costume. Regardless of the reason we end up on our own, there is an intense sense of failure. It wasn't meant to be like this. Then the feelings of inadequacy create a vicious circle: perhaps we are on our own because we deserve to be.

About eight years after Shay died a friend asked why I was still wearing my rings. It was an innocent comment but it caused turmoil in me. The idea of taking my rings off was unthinkable. When I find myself indignant about anything, I know that it tells me more about myself but in this case, I couldn't see what. Eventually I figured that I needed to take off my rings for a few days to see what that felt like. Taking them off was like stripping naked. It was such a painful thing to do but I stuck with it. After about twenty four hours I realised the gift was discovering that Shay wasn't in my rings. They weren't my tiny bit of him to hold on to. He was in my heart; nothing could distort or change that. I kept the rings off for another few days. Once their 'Shay' significance had diluted, I noticed how self-conscious I felt without them. I realised that wearing my rings was also my feeble way of saying to the world, "Look, I was lovable once." Waking up single when I had believed we would grow old together was a huge blow to my self-esteem.

Time heals. I am not as raw missing Shay now. I have become used to the silences that once were our conversations. I can manage on my own, but I am not sure that I want to. It feels like a piece of me has shrivelled dry, as though I have woken up alone on an island. I feel there must be others like me out there, on other islands. It'd be great if we could find each other. This is not about licking wounds. Feck it lads, I don't know about you but I have been miserable in ways for years. I want to give that up. How do we support each other to create fresh ways of being happy?

There are lots of positives already. When I look at my life now, I am chuffed with how independent I have become. In terms of making changes, this was one that life forced on me. I seem to have made the decision not to crumble under the weight of being on my own. It could have gone either way. The question is whether I wait for life to nudge me again or do I take this opportunity to change in new ways that can bring more happiness? To decide what mountain I want to climb or if I can be arsed getting off my backside to do it? I have become more effective in time management. This is a major reason why honest friendship is attractive to me. I love how honesty saves time. Cutting the crap. Listening and learning with an open heart. Laughing at ourselves and daring to get on with whatever presents as the 'point of action'. That moment when we stop thinking about how we would like things to be different; when we get off our backsides to make the change happen.

I need to find a balance between what I want to achieve and what is possible as a single parent. It's different approaching life on my own rather than as a couple. My own parents made a pact years ago. If one of them died, the other would demonstrate the love they had shared by the way they lived on. My Mum has done my Dad proud. Having the world glimpse a little bit of Shay by my actions helps to motivate me too. Daring to be more, to face myself, means that I need someone to mirror me. A bit like one hand clapping, being honest on my own doesn't work as well as when I risk being authentic with friends. That is why it is precious to me to find people who love giving it a go too.

CHAPTER 14

A guru at my table

When I was single, I had plenty of opportunities to consider the big questions in life. It was a time of wonderful adventures. Trekking in Asia, visiting temples, leisurely Saturday morning discussions over coffee, lots of figuring out what I believed might be 'right' answers. Then I met Shay with his son Alan. Loving them meant that Saturdays were suddenly full of washing, ironing and chatting with the neighbours about double glazed windows or schools. Alan was six years old when I first met Shay.

Having grown up beside the sea, I discovered a deep longing for salt air now that we were living inland. I loved being part of family life, but I was hungry for some depth of conversation. Neighbours were very accepting but they would urge me to stop being so serious or thinking so deeply. I tucked that part of myself away, imagining that sometime in the future I would return to the quest to see the bigger picture. Maybe six months in a beachfront ashram when the kids had grown would restore my sense of oneness with the universe. Smelly socks and dirty nappies did little to nurture that part of my soul. I had a sense and a longing that there was a guru 'out there'. I nearly missed one sitting at my table, sharing a cuppa and a gossip.

At the time, Siobhan happily insisted that she had never read a book. She dismissed all of my deep and meaningful nonsense. The fact that I had never frequented the local pub she saw as a serious character flaw. This day, ranting in indignation about some family argument, Siobhan stopped mid-sentence, shed the fury in the blink of an eye and changed the subject. Mystified, I asked her how she did that.

"Ah, I just have to remember about the 'flabby happies'."

Around this time I had been struggling with the idea that people who bug us are gifts in our learning to manage our anger. Flabby happies? Siobhan explained that her house overlooked a church where many of the elderly of the community attend daily mass. From her window she had noticed older women exiting the church with either 'flabby happy' faces or faces like 'hen's arses'. Life was simple: would a reaction lead her to a flabby happy old age or a hen's arse? If something was unlikely to be resolved, she shed it, gratefully protecting herself from pursed lips and squinting eyes in those precious last years of life. Siobhan got that change happens at the point of action, so she just did it. She let go of anger in the blink of an eye, the sort that can stick to me like glue.

I do see people as gifts to my being a better person until they start to really bug me and I just want to smack them. I catch myself. "Breathe deeply. Try to be bigger than this." My impulse is still to smack them! Then what creeps in is the suspicion that the fact I have never hit anyone in my life is half the problem.

What I learnt from the nuns and most female role models in Ireland was to convert anger into a missile that leaves your opponent with a serious dose of guilt. Bullseye! I am good at that.

So what do I teach my kids? I started from a basic premise that 'we don't hit'. Pulling siblings apart, ensuring my voice was quiet yet assured (the parenting books would be proud of me) I insisted 'we don't hit'. Worked great, until my son was being pulverised by a bully in the school yard. Where is the chapter in parenting books with the detail 'if your child needs to hit back in defence, this is the exact amount of force they should use'? Or that says 'sorry mate, buggered if I know what to do'. When I try to get it 'right' by turning the other cheek, I rarely feel fulfilled. It's more that I am left nursing what feels like a black and blue face with grudges that mean I am right on course for a hen's arse. I believe that it makes sense to forgive. I get the 'theory' but find the practise a step too far sometimes.

Since my default position is to people please, I could easily get lost finding new ways to make other people happy, to 'improve' my life that way. How do I make sure that the choices I make are not to impress or for fear of criticism? I realise now that whatever anyone threw at me growing up, I accepted it to be a truth. It might only have been the raise of an eyebrow by a teacher. I believed the implication that there is something wrong with me. A few years ago, someone chided me that I speak too fast. It made me self-conscious so I tried to slow down the way I spoke. I sounded like I had had a stroke. Since then, I have moved to Scotland. One day when I was 'rabbiting' away telling some story (because, of course, I had failed in my resolution to slow down) a new acquaintance offered "You speak very fast. I hope you will come to trust that there is plenty of time. I am happy to listen."

It made such a difference. I wasn't trying to change out of a sense of failure or people pleasing. Changing from a place of confidence that it would serve me better, helped me to see why I can talk so fast. Apart from being Irish! I realised that I fill silences to stop people getting too close. I discovered that one of my addictions is talking. There was a time when embarrassing silences terrified me. Now what disturbs me is whatever prevents a conversation from being real. What is important for me now is for people to say what matters to them. When I hear a beautiful poem or idea, it feels delicious. I love it. But whenever someone speaks his/her truth, it touches something much deeper in me. I change.

CHAPTER 15

What if there is no right or wrong?

What if it's about what works? I'm beginning to grasp that if taking responsibility for my life, choosing what works for me rather than what someone else says works, is a better way forward. The Catholic head in me struggles with this idea. I was brought up with one truth: choices were simply right or wrong. The only variance was whether the 'wrong' was bad enough to land me in hell or just get me a few Hail Marys in confession. Some part of me must have been listening because, in spite of myself, there is such a stranglehold belief that 'wrong is wrong!' Stealing and lying are just wrong. But if my children were starving, I would steal. I'd like to think that I would go back and settle up after the event, but that is from the comfort of my civilised life now. If lying meant that we would have qualified for some treatment that would have saved Shay's life, I'd have lied in a blink, regardless of how much value I place on honesty. A moral code is there to make our lives easier. Honouring it is not a problem as long as it is working. When it fails to meet a situation adequately, what guides us to make the right choices?

When I was nine years old I noticed numbers on the arm of one of my parents' friends. I traced the line with my finger, asking John about his tattoo. He quietly told me of how, aged thirteen, he had entered Auschwitz with his parents and family, what daily life was like and how he was liberated four and a half years later, alone. Silent outrage consumed me. These Nazis were worse than the scariest baddies in stories, this was real. John had basset-hound eyes that watered at the best of times. For a few moments, he and I sat with stereo tears dribbling down. Then John placed his hand on mine and said "We are all the same."

"They were just people trying to survive too. They did what they did. Most of us who managed to come out alive had to commit atrocities to be able to tell the tale today. It's different now, but as a teenager I felt real joy when a truckload of Jews arrived because I knew that being a Polish Catholic, there wouldn't be room in the gas chamber for me that week. I did other things to stay alive as I escaped to Italy, everyone did."

I refused to see my hero as a baddie. He just patted my hand and said "Never forget that we are all the same."

Scientists speak of us being the same as chairs, tables, trees, plastic, atoms and molecules. That same feels interesting. Statements like 'we are all one in the cosmos' I just about get, but only as long as we are all nice ones. I am uncomfortable with the dark side of humanity. I do accept that I have a shadow side but I want to imagine my children with a future that is untainted by any shadow side of theirs. Of course I know they have dark sides. I live with them. But in my world, like nappies, they will grow out of that. When I prepare their bags for school trips, everything is washed and ironed, every eventuality covered. I don't keep a spare rucksack pocket to fill in case they want to pull the legs off spiders. So, before I even start, I'm back to a black and white interpretation. It's about what works, providing it's the 'right' what works. My challenge is the grey areas. I was taught that life was black and white. Grey is simply scrubbed until it reverts to black or white. Cleanliness is next to godliness. But the grey of life is rarely sorted by a bucket and mop.

We have two cats and two dogs. It strikes me that some element of the grey is captured in my attitude to them. Our dogs are fairly well behaved. Everything appears fine until a gate is left open. Suddenly the suggestion that I have any control disintegrates. The cats arrived with no such illusions. With them I realise that the only way forward is to decide my boundaries and live by that. They give what they want to give. I can't manipulate them to make me feel good about myself. I'm realising that with the dogs and my children, I have a sense of investing in the future. Teaching my children to say please and thank you or the dogs to sit is about me creating a nice world for us all. The future always seems more ideal than my life today. The children might develop a desire to do homework, to hoover. The cats force me to live in the real world, now. They suit themselves; they challenge me to consider what suits me. Of course my job as a Mum is to invest in my children's future. The difference is for me to resist any illusion that I can control what unfolds. Treating my children like cats and dogs has limited value and possibly legal implications. Would life be chaotic if we all opted to suit ourselves?

A mate of mine, a dedicated wife and mum, declared one day

that she'd had enough. It had dawned on her that she was entirely responsible for the martyrdom of her life. She quietly vowed that in future she would never do anything that wasn't what she truly wanted to do. Everyone around her seemed to put themselves first so she would see what would happen when she turned the tables on them. She waited for the backlash from her family, especially her husband. Weeks later, realising that his strategy had been to ignore her antics, she demanded;

"Okay, tell the truth. What have you really thought about my choosing what I want to do, rather than trying to keep all of you happy?"

Her husband looked mystified.

"You mean you haven't always been doing what you wanted to do?"

What stops me from owning what I want and including that equally in my priorities? I was brought up to believe that putting me first is selfish. Particularly being a girl, my job is to give of myself. But if I take this too far then there is very little of me to give. How can I be generous-hearted and include me in the equation? I need my children to understand they matter but that they are not the centre of everyone else's universe. That finding real joy is about taking command of their own lives. To choose to make their own health their priority; realising that self-esteem is crucial to good health. A definition of self-esteem is 'believing you are capable and believing you are lovable'. I'd sell a kidney if I thought that I could buy self-esteem for my kids. I can buy them education, a house, a car, but not the life to live in them. I look to theories suggesting answers to the big questions of life hoping they might be the map I have been looking for. I don't seem to get very far.

An example of where I get stuck is the Buddhist philosophy that 'life is an illusion'. I deeply respect that many people live exemplary lives in this belief. I've tried it on for size but to date, I don't get it. Not up close. So yet again, I phoned my friend Anne who 'gets these things'; an amazing woman who has read as much as I have eaten. Much of our friendship has been snatched phone conversations in between the joys of family life.

"Anne, this is wrecking my head. I don't get that life is an illusion".

Someone had been insistent that this was all I needed to have perfect peace. Peace me arse, it was driving me nuts.

"Next time you see them, hold them gently by the shoulders, look them lovingly in the eyes and kick them hard on the shins. Then smile and say 'that's an illusion'."

Anne needed to race back to some family demand. I held the phone in a 'eureka' moment. Now that I get!

I see Buddhists like the Dalai Lama. I sense that they grasp the truth of life being an illusion. It looks so attractive, real happiness. I would love it. But, as with the distance from the back of the class to the teachers' good books, I'm not sure what stops me getting there. It feels too far. Trying to impart that depth of contentment to teens when I don't have it myself is a helluva place to start.

CHAPTER 16

I need somewhere new to start from

Some wonderful and some very warped women tried to guide me to discover the divinity inside myself: I was convent-educated in Ireland. Wrath-filled warnings of good and bad, right and wrong. My priority has been to avoid giving the kids the hang-ups we were given. It is dawning on me that they need more. I now have sympathy for my parents and the nuns trying to communicate 'important lessons'. If fear of damnation would get my children to behave, I might try it on for size. But this generation is not worried about Satan or the bogeyman. They have beaten much worse in virtual games. They worry about belonging with their peers more than they worry about getting into trouble when they get home. I am realising that in my effort to teach them not to feel guilty, I have also taught them not to feel very responsible.

We were given an inadequate map to cope with life, one that fell short of our needs in the real world. Instead of creating a better map, we seem to have created an artificial world where every boy can be a virtual hero and every girl a sparkly pink princess. It's wonderful that they believe in themselves that much but where is the substance in it to carry them in real life? We were dragged to church to try to address this one. I can't imagine that forcing my two to daily Rosary and Benediction would work, though I love the idea that girls need some type of religion, if only to believe there is something bigger than themselves when they hit their teens. Where do our children belong? I was told that I belonged with Catholicism until such time that I died or was excommunicated.

Excommunication is when the Pope advises his equivalent of nightclub bouncers to escort you off the premises with the instruction never to return. My first introduction to this possibility was when I was four years old. My grandmother was babysitting. We were all in our pyjamas, ready for bed, when she brought us together to say our night-time prayers. Kneeling on linoleum in front of a tall mahogany crucifix, we began five decades of the rosary. We usually had kitchen chairs to lean against so it was particularly difficult to keep still. Granny began with a series of prayers of thanks. One was for the day we had enjoyed. My mind wandered to the school yard. I had recently started school. There were about a thousand children in the yard. I was still in shock. There were 45 children in my own class; one hundred and eighty in my year of four years olds, all at sea. That day had been great fun though. I had arrived to school with a new joke. I had the pleasure of sending the ripple around the yard.

My joke was friendly and simple so it had been well received. I had approached my school mates, instructing them to 'be an aeroplane'. They dutifully put their arms in the air, waiting for the next command. Instead, I reached up to tickle under their arms. We loved it. School was good that day. In my reverie I shifted my knees on the lino. As I resettled myself, I obediently focused on the statue in front of me. I noticed something I had never had the joy to notice before. Jesus on the crucifix was in aeroplane mode. At first it was enough to harbour the realisation to myself. It was delicious to include Jesus in the fun of the day. It cheered up the rosary; I was happily distracted for a few more decades of prayers. I was four years old, the anticipation got the better of me. I reached up to tickle Jesus. All hell broke loose.

I hadn't expected a statue to chuckle but I certainly didn't expect the hellfire and brimstone that ensued. My brothers were sent to bed. I spent hours on my knees with my grandmother praying for my soul. In those days having a secure credit balance on your soul was the only way to survive life or death. I could buy back forgiveness by praying for my sins. My job was to behave or to buy back his favour when I didn't. Credit and debit. I clearly was in debt. Some of the older kids in the yard had dismissed our game as too babyish. I would have understood if Jesus had seen it as childish. It was a surprise to discover that it was deemed the work of the devil, that this Jesus bloke definitely didn't have a sense of humour. It took until I was thirty before it occurred to me that Jesus might have laughed.

It has been a journey to learn not to take life so seriously. One of the greatest gifts as a child was sitting in the back of a pal's car as her father changed lanes randomly. Wide-eyed, I'd hear horns beeping indignantly, then his voice as he would contentedly announce, "Feck them if they can't take a joke!"

Often, when I have made a mistake, I have walked away with the echo of his words carrying me up out of the abyss of self-flagellating guilt. In recent years, I have found myself adding, "Feck them, I wouldn't even hug them!"

When I was a teen I was hungry for honesty but it mattered more to fit in. There are levels of transparency that adolescents don't do very easily. I lived under the limits set by peers but the thirst for answers remained. It showed itself in trying to figure out what was authentic in what the adults fed us. Much of the dogma in religion wrecked my head. The contradictions felt like lies. The nuns told me to look to Mary for guidance as a woman. The only way that was going to work was if I decided celibacy was a game plan. The nuns stood in front of Mary's sexless statue in their sexless robes and told us Mary had the answers for our sex. I definitely had questions, but Mary seemed a very unsatisfactory place to look for any answers to my womanhood. Whether she had them or not, something freed up in me when it dawned that she probably had stretch-marks. I felt lighter, happier. It felt like a truth. A straight connection in to my substance suggesting that it was okay for me to be a real woman, that Mary had been one. It makes me hope that she knew what an orgasm was. It seems fine to think of her as possibly sneezing, of her going through the intense feelings of watching her son dying but it is strangely taboo to think of her in joy.

I was in my twenties before I realised that guilt is meant to protect us. That I was only meant to feel it once, to warn me that this behaviour is not in my best interests. It's not meant to linger like a bad smell. The nuns unwittingly threw the equivalent of stink bombs at us, the odour penetrated our beings. They called it humility. Another surprise for me is that 'shame is someone else's guilt'. It is as inappropriate as picking up the wrong coat and walking away in it until registering that this particular stench isn't of your making. In Ireland, we tend to hold on to the coat, layer it on top of what we are already wearing and smile a lot, trying to distract people from the fact that we have serious shame odour.

I don't want to teach my children to feel that true happiness in their souls is something they can 'buy' with good behaviour or lose by not following rules. They need to dig deeper than that. Yet, if a child is distressed there is usually the sound of a shop till or food packaging involved in the answer. What my children seem to have picked up is that as long as they have money they will be capable, as long as they know how to be cool they will be lovable. They have a distorted confidence in what they perceive 'works' for them.

When Brian was born, a card suggested 'to love him is to teach him to love that which is difficult'. With the utter conviction of a first time mum who had been raised with the idea that doing something the 'right way' would inevitably mean that it would have to be difficult, I committed faithfully to this. Life soon took over. I quickly forgot any of my greater aspirations in the seductive tones of my children cooing contentedly. The hum of children playing is one of the sweetest sounds to me. Loving my children felt like I was doing my job at last. Looking back I realise that a considerable amount of the cooing came from purchases that required little of me as an adult or minimal creativity on their part. I tried to choose educational toys but marketing meant that they soon begged for the 'other' ones. Their glazed zombie eyes asked less of me.

On reflection overall, I have detached them from some of the experience of living by creating a cocoon. As a mum, a cocoon around my babies feels like a good thing. It's difficult to give it up. It feels like I am protecting them from the hard edges of life. But when they mature into adults there is a good chance the cocoon will shatter. Life hits everyone in the face sometime. I need to make sure that their knee jerk reaction is not to try to buy their happiness back. What if what I taught them means that credit cards or substance abuse become their gurus? Eventually in debt, they may awaken (if they are lucky) to realising that they are responsible for their own lives. The first step towards finding their real power, but having left a trail of heartbreak and hard lessons along the way.

All the 'mammy' efforts to protect my children from feeling their discomfort meant that I could avoid mine too as we were up to our tonsils grieving Shay. By tucking them into their car seats, singing merry songs on the way to the toy shop, everyone was happy. It worked. Well, for fifteen minutes at least. Hearing quiet happy children made my day seem worthwhile. Cheap at the price. The problem is that our children seem to be the ones who carry the cost. So if I haven't taught my children self-esteem, what have they learnt? It is dawning on me that what I have handed down is potentially the grassroots of addiction.

CHAPTER 17

Adam and Eve were raving alcoholics...

...on cider from the apples! I figure that is where avoiding the truth started. There isn't a family on the planet that has escaped the joys of addiction. We Irish do it particularly well. Drink, drugs and gambling are the most visible forms. I believe that addiction is what happens when we don't know what to do with the grey of life, so we try to stuff it back down. One of my turning points in making sense of my own life came when I heard about the different 'roles' that we play in families. It has been a fantastic help to me in understanding why I react the way I do. Recognising my patterns has been easier than actually changing them!

How do we break habits such as the times we sit around dunking choccy biscuits in cuppas, whining about our lives or our weight? That can be great fun until it is not. When life demands more, we risk stewing in pain if we don't find a better way to move forward. When I began to grasp the dynamics of my addictive tendencies, it struck me that Adam and Eve probably got the ball rolling. Addiction is rooted in whatever we use to avoid uncomfortable emotions. We either deal with hurt when it happens, or it lies dormant until it comes back to bite our bums. Most of us learnt as kids to tuck it away so as to avoid dealing with it. The following is my attempt to capture what I understand about 'roles in families'. I'm including it because I feel it is what drives the choices that I make when I am faced with the possibility of peace and joy but somehow end up in a less blissful state. Lots of my friends who want to change something in their lives also have addiction in their families. This is a place where we have discovered common ground, understanding how each of us play the addiction card too.

When did we first learn to stuff feelings back down? Chances are that everything was going fine for Adam and Eve until the pressures of being banished got to them. I figure that the apples probably fermented because Eve had her hands full and she forgot to put them in the shade. Adam and Eve began to nark at each other. Their children looked up to ask what was wrong. From the moment that either parent told them "nothing, go back and play", the *10 commandments of how not to cope with life* were laid down, starting with:

1. Do not trust (because at least one of these adults is not telling the truth!)
2. Do not talk (unless you enjoy getting your head bitten off!)
3. Do not feel (because that was what caused you to ask the question!)

So, doing as they were told, they returned to playing. They looked fine on the outside, but their sense that there was something wrong in the world remained. The confusion and fear in their tummies looked for a place to find peace. The eldest possibly realised that by being 'good', the initial growls from parents became looks of appreciation. It worked. So he herded the other children, making sure they were safe. This left space for the parents to recover from their own distress, with murmurings of "That lad has never been a day's bother."

No surprise that when he grew up he became the first social worker.

In every family, the order that we take on the roles can vary but each role tends to play out in the same way. I'm connecting roles to employment because they have a tendency to lead to certain lifestyle choices, like the way that people in caring professions often have a strong need to be needed. They learnt early to rescue; to feel good about themselves by making other people feel good. Having an overview helps us see the patterns of how we cope. In turn, it helps us embrace the idea that 'my greatest strength can be my greatest weakness and my greatest weakness can be my greatest strength.'

The second child decided to impress. A deft climber, he scaled the trees bringing home a bounty of coconuts. His productivity made the family look normal. He was a credit to his parents. He grew up needing lots of recognition. He started the first circus.

The third child, left with anger boiling inside, opted for destruction. When no one was looking, she released her pent up emotions by smashing the food stores. This got her copious attention. It didn't matter to her that her parents were raving at her. At least they were looking in her direction. Impulsive behaviour worked on many levels. Firstly, it prompted the parents to have to talk to each other when they had been avoiding contact. For her, there was less stuffing emotions back down so much as letting go and making it someone else's problem. It worked! Discovering the pleasures of fermented fruit, she eventually became the first person to attend rehab.

The fourth child, the 'scapegoat', was deeply unhappy about the avoidance of truth. She insisted there was something wrong between her parents, thereby incurring further wrath from them. This made her withdraw with the conviction that only truth would assuage her pain. She formed the first workers' union when she grew up.

The last child ignored everyone, wandering off to escape into his imagination. Dispelling the pain in his gut by staring at the stars and fantasising about another life altogether. Chances are he had his wishes fulfilled since wandering around the jungle wistfully focusing on stars means there is a good chance he became a tiger's dinner rather than grow up. And that brings us to another of the commandments of how not to cope with life:

4.   A measure of addiction is that the end result can be death.

Fairly obvious with cirrhosis of the liver or heroin overdose but more subtle with the first son (the hero). Obsessed with saving the world, he developed hypertension and had a heart attack at 35 years of age. At his funeral all the mutterings were that 'only the good die young' (presumably at that stage they had limited statistics to go on). He died an addicted co-dependent, needing to be needed. He also started the trend that seeming to give to the tribe is rarely considered addiction by the tribe.

The second son (the mascot – whose achievements made the family look good) had several opportunities at death; his ego meant that he refused safety nets in his high flying performance. In fact, he died of a sexually transmitted disease as he exploited his fame to satisfy a sex addiction.

The third (the problem child) had discovered early that venting feelings is a better way to go. Not before she developed several addictions to mood altering drugs. Ostracised by her family, she nurtured friendships with the chimps who she taught to join her in taking alcohol and drugs. One day, she woke up with the worst hangover and decided to change her ways. Her detox centre for chimps and apes was a great success. Often 'the problem' is the one who actually finds health.

Her sister (the scapegoat), who searched for the one true path, got clobbered to death by warring factions who turned on her when she tried to intercede between tribes and bring peace. Her epitaph read 'Don't give them the answers until they ask the questions.' Very few people want the real truth. They buried her beside her tiger eaten brother (the lost child).

5. Instead of dealing with pain, the way to cope with life is to 'control' situations before they can hurt us.

6. The best way to control is to be purist about right and wrong behaviours. Being judgemental is the way to go. Black and white is the new black.

7. The 'grey of life' is the root of all evil. To be avoided whenever possible.

8. When life spirals out of control, an acceptable way to cope is to be impulsive.

9. Whatever we become addicted to, the need for it increases rather than lessens.

10. The measure of how addicted we are, is how emotionally unavailable we are to those around us.

My Dad was a good man, but as a teen I thought the funniest Father's Day card was one with a hole cut out of the inside page so that he could watch the TV while he read the card! Our kids accept our addictive behaviours as normal. We tell them not to smoke, drink, take drugs, stay too long on the computer... but they watch much better than they listen.

So the daughters of Eve and sons of Adam gave us the '10 commandants of how not to cope with life'. Like all of us they developed these strategies to survive childhood, to make sense of their world. It was when they continued dealing with life in the same way as adults that the real effect was felt.

CHAPTER 18

A map of the grey

All of us behave like Adam and Eve's clan. We tend to take one role in the family but we tick all the boxes in different ways. When we were children, feelings surfaced in response to events. If we got a message that they weren't okay then we found ways to push them down to a manageable size. Children are survivors. How we behaved was a direct product of how we experienced the adults around us.

Religion tried to show us the way by filling in any gaps left. Lots of black and white. Simple solutions to the big questions; sex, drugs, homosexuality were wrong. We didn't know who we were, but we got really good at being or looking like who they wanted us to be. I left school and college not having a clue who I was or what I wanted. I'd settle for my children knowing who they really are. It's easy to find what will bring us life when we have an idea who we are. Friends who pay attention to what makes them feel joy rarely dread Monday mornings. They also seem to be more comfortable about where the 'grey' fits into their life.

'Grey' for me was the territory of Shay's diagnosis. We had thought that by being good, only good things would happen to us. We woke up in a nightmare with very few tools to tell us what to do. One option was to do what we were told, but if Shay had been 'good' then he would have missed eighteen months of life. If it is not just about being good, what can we teach our children? One of the best pieces of advice Grace will ever receive was from a doctor who uses complementary medicine alongside her years of medical experience. In the middle of a consultation she stopped to ask Grace "what are you good at?"

Grace muttered "music."

"You need to do more music. Lots of it. This is crucial for your health."

Imagine if someone had told us as kids to put our hearts and souls into what we were good at rather than to just be good.

When I was nine years of age, I had an essay read out in school. I was thrilled at the time. Over the years it seemed as though it must have been a fluke. No other English teacher seemed to see anything of worth. Instead there were lots of concerns about poor grammar and spelling. 'Could do better' was the best compliment I ever received in a school report. Ever since, I have been self-conscious about how poor I am at writing. Now, attempting this, I'm giving the bits that I seem to be able to do a go. I find I have joy in my heart that I only ever felt in Shay's arms or holding the kids in mine. All I have to offer is to be honest on paper while reaching out in friendship. It is a surprise to me how alive I feel. Most of the writing of this has taken place at about 4am, facing into hectic days. It has exhausted me but it has never once felt like work. The laundry that waits downstairs would probably take thirty minutes to clear, but feels like a pain in the ass of responsibility.

Grace gets her music from Shay. He was 34 years old when he discovered that he had it in him. With the inheritance from his Mum he bought himself a guitar. It became obvious that he had a natural talent. All three of his children have this. It meant so much to him to nurture it in them. How different his life might have been if he had known that he could play when he was young. It might have been a safe place to shed feelings in the midst of his Dad dying.

After his own diagnosis, Shay attended a handful of art classes as a way to relax. There he discovered that this was natural to him too. Clearing the house since, I came across a painting of Shay's which had won first place in a Texaco art competition when he was eight years of age. Yet years later, it was a surprise to him that he did so well at the classes he attended. Finding and nurturing our joy matters.

CHAPTER 19

The F word

What if farts hold some of the answers? Initially, they were where I found my God. It dawned on me that if Mary had stretch marks... Jesus must have farted. In fact, every incarnate representative we have of the divine must have let a trump. Over time farting has become a measure of real friendship for me, depending on how comfortable I feel with someone when I accidentally fart. We all fart: rarely, thankfully, but the 'what if' helps me to have a sense of the integrity of a relationship. We either opt for 'let's pretend nothing is happening' which leaves me clinging on to the hope that they may not have noticed... or we can choose to connect in the honesty of the moment. A gentle grin of shared recognition and acceptance.

I am hungry to find more of the softer connection, preferably without the 'wind' factor. It leads me to deeply appreciate 'farting acquaintances' – those friendships where I know I am always accepted, wind, warts, stretch-marks and all. A part of me feels self-conscious to be writing about farts. I wish that I could find a different way to say the same thing, but that is the potency of this. A 'no go' area where we all go. In reality it's fab that farts refuse to be contained. If we manage to suppress them in public, they release as soon as we are out of sound and smelling distance. Whereas, when we cover up feelings they can get stuck there. Farts are something we all do. Farts are something we all hide. Farts help us to feel better (although those around us may need a little recovery time).

Feelings are a bit like farts. They are a part of human nature, they are something we all hide and we are happier when we are not trying to keep them in. Feelings can help us to make choices, they can direct us to find what brings us life. When Shrek declares "better out than in" it makes us grin because he is speaking to a need in all of us. It is the simple truth that it is vital to our wellbeing and happiness to shed rather than hold on to our waste products. What if all the loos in the world disappeared? Imagine walking around trying to hide the fact that you desperately need one. What a daft thing to do. Yet we do it all the time with feelings.

The reason I started writing this book is that I want more peace and joy in our lives. The question is whether 'coming out' as a person who farts is likely to achieve that. The issue is not the fart or the feeling. It is what we have learnt to do to suppress them, to hide them from ourselves and others. The 'learning' is a crucial element. As babies, we arrived into the world knowing what to do to keep happy and healthy. Then we were told not to do it.

They replaced our intuitive knowing about how to cope by teaching us to judge emotions.

"Boys don't cry and girls should be nice and never get angry"

Feelings are not good or bad, they just are. I was taught that anger was a 'bad' feeling. Now I realise that I have a right to my anger, but it doesn't give me rights. Most of all I realise that staying stuck in it distracts me from what is really going on. So, 'good or bad' is the way that we hold in or release feelings, not the feelings themselves. When I am hurting and my impulse is to lash out; I need to remember that no matter how much I hurt someone, my own hurt does not lessen. I want to arrive at a place where my default is to let off steam in the moment, rather than stuffing it back down, preventing my 'pressure cooker erupting' quality.

Steam can turn turbines or scald. It is a choice. I remember standing back to consider a kitchen refurbishment that I completed the year after Shay died. It meant that I could see the children in the garden as they played outside. It was a lovely, welcoming 'everyone wants to be in the kitchen' space. Intrigued as to how I had managed it, I realised that anger had been my main driving force. I was so upset that Shay had died, I couldn't sleep. Not knowing what to with the churning ache inside, I got busy. I love that it brought some good.

I used to be afraid of strong feelings. If someone got angry, deep down I was scared that somehow their letting off steam might annihilate me. I did all in my power to stop that happening. I developed a clown-like facial expression that seemed to tell the world I was not a threat. It was my survival strategy. It usually deterred people from attacking me, but it didn't stop me being fearful that they might. It was a breakthrough for me when I realised that people don't actually want to hurt us. All they are doing is trying to offload their own hurt by pushing it away from themselves, whether they are letting off wind or letting off their pain by ranting. The end product is not meant for us, even though it feels as if we are the target sometimes.

Shay's dying is the nearest to annihilation that I ever want to get. I can only imagine that something happening to the kids could ever push me further. I have survived. It took more than demented grinning. I couldn't appease death by a submissive stance. It came, hit me in the face; I am still standing. Now when anything happens, I unconsciously measure it against Shay dying. Once it hurts less than that, I am not scared anymore. Since the Holocaust, there is a Jewish saying:

"Of this, children do not burn to death."

Sometimes we make life more complicated than it really is. Having survived losing Shay, the rest of life seems a bit of a doddle. Letting out a few feelings isn't that big a deal.

Mind you, I have no desire to contaminate every room that I enter with the potency of the gas in my gut or to have supressed feelings contaminate all of my life. That means finding safe places to shed them. The first time I took ownership of a fart, I looked the person straight in the face and said "my apologies that was me". It shifted the way we communicated, the person grinned comfortably and we continued chatting. There was a tangible sense of more integrity and trust there. I don't go around farting on purpose. But if one slips out, I try to own it. Not everyone is as easy going, but I love the friendships that are – my farting acquaintances. This book is essentially looking to develop 'feelings acquaintances', to move past the way that underneath our smiles and small talk, we all have emotions that are being kept in place for fear of showing. I want friendships where there is space to own feelings instead of trying to pretend that they don't exist so we can move through whatever dragging us down instead of carrying extra baggage around all the time.

Holding feelings back rarely fools people. You know that vague whiff that happens when there is a tiny leak of a failed 'held in' fart. Or the times when any of us think we are hiding our feelings; that we are fooling everyone from what is going on inside of us. A pal slapped my back in friendship recently. I was left with an acute sense that beneath her smiles, her high pitched insistence that all was well, was a depth of hurt that left my back stinging. My two lived with my leaking anger and sadness for years. Stuffing my pain back down was confusing to them. It undermined their childhood confidence that letting go of feelings is the better way to deal with life. How is it that we lose that knowing? The wisdom of the body works hard to get rid of waste products, my gut finds 'peace' when it releases gas. Once it is gone, it's gone. I have no impulse to hold on to or collect farts or to be able to take a jar out every so often, to smell that smell again. Farts definitely belong in the past. Yet I waste time collecting feelings, holding on to old dramas of my life or imagining ones in the future.

Farts and feelings respond to similar spaces to 'air'. When I hit a wide open beach, all I am holding inside releases into the atmosphere. I don't really notice its departure. It's later, when I feel clean and refreshed, I notice that nature has done its thing. I love the way that the wind has blown my cobwebs away. Any time we get to spend in nature, the 'nature' in us begins to gently release what we are holding. The more I do it, the more I seem to thrive. The intelligence of my body knows how to fix me whenever I stop getting in its way.

There was a serious 'fart factor' when Shay dealt with his disappointment of the likelihood of managing a 'cure'. Once he had declined further chemotherapy, his only regret was having allowed it to go straight to the top of his list of treatment options when he was diagnosed. He had had four rounds of 96 hours of chemo over a four month period before he refused any more. He would go in on Monday morning and have continual chemo until Friday evening. In Shay's case, it did nothing to affect the cancer but it devastated his body. Along with the avoidable septicaemia from the Hickman, it meant that he had much less to work with when he dared to dream. Shay raged against the disappointment of this. He needed to explode, to release what felt like the injustice of it all. We asked family to take the kids out. I brought Shay home from the hospital for a few hours at the tail-end of his admission for the septicaemia. It gave him time and space to go into meltdown. Letting out feelings stops us from imploding. The release played a major part in him living a further fifteen months against all expectation.

Usually women seem to find it easier to be honest about feelings. Men find it easier to be honest about farts. It's great when we can learn from each other. Kids' tend not to be too concerned about either; their default position is to presume that life is fun. They delight at the smallest moments. Kids love farts! Kids are not easily taken in. Yet somehow in our day I feel we were. For Shay, shedding feelings rather than keeping them bottled inside helped to bring him more than a year extra of life. He got to see his daughter take her first steps, witness Alan's buzz as he formed a band with mates, and be there for Brian's first day of school. It took courage. The rewards were priceless.

CHAPTER 20

The T in fart...

It's less about making a smell and more about showing up in the 'truth' of farts or feelings. Truth can be scary to face; when I risk it, I notice how much lighter and easier life feels. Honesty always feels 'cleaner' than the alternative for me. I have chosen to be honest for a long time. What is becoming clear is that there is a quality to this which is more than being good and telling the truth. Honesty isn't enough, unless it includes being honest with ourselves. We all know decent folk whose word we can trust. Good, upstanding people. But if they are not speaking what is true for them, there is a heaviness, a lack of joy. In school we were told to tell the truth but we were discouraged from speaking our truth.

In Brian's first school, there was a system of green and orange cards for behaviour. Green was given in recognition of good behaviour and orange was a marker of bad behaviour. Brian could have wallpapered our house with green cards. Wonderful, except his Dad wasn't long dead. I asked the teachers if they thought it strange that he wasn't kicking other kids on the shins. The teachers rolled their eyes in exasperation at how parents are never happy, reassuring me that he was an excellent pupil. Eventually, I discerned that Brian was afraid to do anything bad in case something else bad happened. So, in my view, success for him would be orange cards. I sent him off each day urging him to get at least one. He never managed it. But those that I looked to for approval gave me thumbs up, seeing him as a roaring success. What is true for us is not necessarily true for someone else.

Stepping into honesty starts by taking a close look at what I believe as my truth, then adding in a pinch of salt. What I perceive as true for me could easily get lost in me perceiving life as 'happening to me'. The outcome is different when I own whatever comes my way by recognising that it was my choice. Initially I struggled with the idea that I am volunteer rather than victim of all of my life. We never 'chose' for bad things to happen. We were rear ended in a car accident in 1993. We didn't pack the car that morning planning to have the car written off in the afternoon. But we did choose to be on that road that day though. What am I choosing now? I am beginning to recognise that every moment of my life can be traced back to a choice I have made. It gives hope because it means that I have choice in what becomes 'true' for me in the future.

The only element to choice I haven't quite gotten my head around is how it works for children. Alan, Brian and Grace didn't want their Dad to die. Where was their choice? By falling in love with Shay, I risked being his widow. They were born into this. Those who believe in reincarnation suggest that we start making choices before we decide to come back down again. We choose our path for the lessons we need to learn this time around. This idea appeals to me, especially for those times when the kids are on my case. I like the option of shrugging off my responsibility as a parent by declaring "apparently it's your fault... you chose me."

Being honest with children can be a challenge. We want to protect them. The day Shay was diagnosed was Brian's fourth birthday. The house was suddenly full of people who weren't there for his party. Brian wanted to know what was happening. I explained that the doctor had told us that Daddy had a fight on his hands that everyone had come to help him. The following night, settling into bed, Brian asked me, "What if Daddy doesn't win the fight?"

Taking a deep breath, I tried to explain what was happening. It felt too soon.

"If Daddy doesn't win the fight, then Daddy would go to heaven. He would pass away."

Tears dribbled down my face as I walked back downstairs. He was too young for this much reality. The next morning I was woken by an irate child standing by my bed with his hands on his hips.

"Mammy, you know the goldfish that died a few weeks ago? Well it died dead, it didn't just pass away and go to heaven."

Kids know the truth even when we can't bring ourselves to say it.

I was doing my best at the time. Brian needed more. I care to attempt the more, but there are qualities about authentic that I have yet to master. It feels like if I can land there; there is more fun to be had. Up until now, my choosing honesty in my life was because I had come to hate the loneliness of deceit. I had spent most of my own childhood and teens telling lies when it would have been as easy to tell the truth. My motivation came from not believing that I was enough. Once I started liking myself after years of not, lying became irrelevant and cumbersome. It was such a relief when I decided to stop. I'd have stopped way sooner if I had known that it would feel so good. Most behaviours that I'd like to change are the same. It is less about the right or wrong of them and more about my needing to pay attention to what drives them, starting with having the courage to face whatever I unearth.

A place that I have noticed the payoff of honesty is in my kids. My baseline is to presume that there is a load I could do better as a parent. Considering all that they have been through, it amazes me how sorted they are. I would understand if they were smearing faeces on the ceiling. Now, the two youngest face their teens without their Dad. I had an angst-driven, unhappy adolescence so I presumed that they would too. They have their angst moments, their concerns, but they also seem to have a solid trust in life and in my love for them. I am deeply grateful for this. I am not sure what ingredient made the difference. All I have had to offer them was me and to show up in honesty.

As a single parent with the same big dreams that Shay and I shared for the family, I am a little battle worn. Where do I go from here? This is me reaching out to the people who recognise that we are not alone at the back of the class. Often the kids at the rear grasped the truth of what was really going on. Together we heard the teacher, saw the lips moving, and the 'bright' kids' heads nodding in understanding. All the while, I was stuck in one of the back rows staring out the window.

CHAPTER 21

"No one ever got drunk on an intellectual understanding of wine"

Many of my life lessons didn't happen in the classroom at all. My favourite was from a housewife in 1980. I was 19 years old. We attended the same gym. At that time in Ireland, men and women had separate gyms. Even then, all the women queued to change in the only cubicle that had a curtain. We chatted happily waiting for our turn, ignoring the five other empty cubicles. After the workout we all headed to the sauna. Our modesty was assured by vice like knots in our towels. We baked in the steam. One evening, a wonderful woman, Doreen, entered the sauna with a sweep. She climbed up to the top shelf, whipped off her towel and lay down, declaring, "Hiya folks, I'm here to make you all feel adequate."

Ten minutes later, the towels shed, the sauna rang with

laughter and banter. We had great craic! Often since, I have gathered the nerve to enter a party or event trusting that, at my worst 'I'm here to make them all feel adequate'. Up until then, a zit could define me. Somehow, my whole body would seem to become the spot. All my energy and attention would be focused there. It was excruciating trying to socialise when all I was a pimple or a bad hair style or a panty line on my jeans. Now, my being relaxed encourages others. It's a formula that works. I like formulas that work. Lots of the famous and impressive ones don't transfer so easily for me.

I need my goals to be straightforward, simple and real. I need to be confident they are based in experience. In the past, I have turned myself inside out on the advice of anyone that I decided had more answers than I do. Life's mountains are hard enough to climb. Following what other people think, instead of what my own gut tells me, has been more like attempting the summit in high heels, blindfolded and backwards. I give my power away easily. How do I discern the good stuff? For me, trusting that the person knows what they are talking about is crucial. Too often, I have handed over my power because I presumed someone was an 'expert'.

Soon after Shay died, friends were visiting. Grace started crying uncontrollably. I brought her to my bedroom trying to soothe her in my arms. She screamed, spat, clawed and ranted, pushing me away. Twenty minutes later there was no change. I gave up trying to placate her. I sat up on the bed with my arms open. Suddenly she was curled up in my embrace with the residual sobbing that comes after a ripper of a good cry. I wished that I had known to step back sooner.

The next day, I phoned the bereavement team in the hospice for advice. I didn't know if this was the floodgates of her pain opening or that maybe this was just what she had needed, a one-off. I got through to a young, friendly social worker. As I described my daughter's pain, this very young female voice sounded perplexed. She began focussing on the details.

"How long exactly did she do this for? And you are sure this was the first time. Hmmm, you are sure it was for twenty minutes, a full twenty minutes?"

It seemed as though she was ticking boxes of some theory that would possibly diagnose my child as a budding psychopath. A cold, icy hand squeezed at my heart. As a Mum I could only swallow deeply, preparing to take it on the chin. Shay was dead; my chin felt wobbly. Suddenly the social worker apologised that she needed to be at a meeting, that she would refer this to her senior. Someone would phone me back. I sat staring at the phone, wanting to scream.

"I don't think I can take any more".

All the while the mammy voice in my head was "of course you will, you have to." But I was scared that this time I might not be able to.

When the phone rang, a soft male voice asked for me.

"What seems to be the problem?"

It felt like a trick question. Surely his colleague had flagged up that a juvenile psychopath was hatching in front of our eyes. I tried to sound responsible, in control. It dawned on me that, now a single parent, they might consider taking Grace away if they thought I wasn't coping. It felt like someone was stripping the muscles straight off my bones. I kept my voice even.

"My daughter had an outburst yesterday for twenty minutes. I couldn't placate her. I phoned for advice on whether this was normal considering our circumstances."

His reply was considered.

"Twenty minutes, two years old, her Daddy died three months ago."

He continued "Well, my own daughter used to have similar outbursts for over an hour at that age. She had both her parents. It sounds completely normal. You did a great job handling it".

From the moment I put the phone down, I vowed to be wary of anyone giving me parenting advice that hasn't had a child, no matter how many qualifications or good intentions they may bring.

Like most parents, I can do guilt in a blink. I marvel at people who can reach a meditative state in a moment by setting their attention to it. I find it hard to truly relax after an hour of trying, but I am champion at guilt. It switches on like a light bulb, burning from my chest to my gut. At a time when we were struggling to recover, being fed a formula based on theory only caused more trauma. Whereas the dad who happened to be a social worker drew from what he knew to be true. This put meat back on my bones. His honest kindness wrapped me in hope.

I know that the young social worker meant well. Before I had Brian, I used to work in the health system. I wish that I could go back to apologise to everyone that I left scarred when I thought I was doing a great job. Somewhere, there is a woman who had a toddler with Down's Syndrome and a new baby when I was in my early twenties. I can still hear my tut-tutting that she hadn't followed through on the recommended exercise programme for the toddler. Whenever I have been up for three nights with a sick child, I have flashbacks to the incredulity on her face, her blinking back tears. Standing in front of my kitchen sink, with fungus growing on abandoned dishes, I think of her and hope she has the satisfaction of knowing that it took till now but 'I get it'. I'm truly sorry.

CHAPTER 22

Our map of the grey

Facing the grey of life challenges us to develop our own formulas to live. This means living with the consequences. An example of how Shay and I 'lived the grey' was judged by others as irresponsible. The summer Grace was born there was an initiative that meant fathers could take ten weeks unpaid parental leave. We were seriously broke at that time. It seemed a preposterous idea. Shay was clear that he wanted to support Alan during important exams. The school was a drive away so he wanted to be on hand for the different timetable and to help with revision. Shay also wanted to help Brian adjust to sharing Mammy with the new baby. We opted for the parental leave. We understood the reactions by family. They were appalled that we even considered it; it was seen as verging on 'new age' ridiculous. Having planned a homebirth (our second), there had been an air of worry for us before we even mentioned the 'ten weeks off' idea. All the concern was fuelled by caring, wanting to protect us. With only one wage coming into the house, there seemed to be too many demands to risk the madness of giving that up. Shay having the 'good boy' streak could easily have succumbed to the pressure of disapproval.

Nothing brought him more peace and joy than his family though. Shay figured we needed him; that was enough. We decided to take the risk. For ten 'new baby in the house' weeks we had a wonderful time. It still seemed ludicrous to most around us. The sort of boundary-less behaviour that could only bring trouble. What surprised us was that Shay didn't have much energy after ten weeks of rest, so he went for a check-up. The diagnosis hit. Choosing those ten weeks meant the best and most precious holiday we ever had. No money could buy the sweetness of all the picnics in the park or back garden. Whenever we had a 'busy with the baby' night we would simply opt for an easy day, loving the fact that Shay wasn't rushing off to work. Once Alan's exams were finished, he would sit with his baby sister stretched out in front of him on his arms, both Shay and himself listening to Led Zeppelin – Grace's first lessons in music appreciation. My lasting impression of those ten weeks is how often Shay and I grinned at each other.

So now, without Shay to grin at, how do I discern what works in our lives? Friendship helps me see the wood for the trees. Fresh friendships can challenge me to stretch out of the familiar. Older friendships can thrive on the new energy of moving forward. It is so seductive when we witness friends finding happiness. It feels tangible because we know how miserable they were before and now their eyes are smiling and we want some. Sometimes, growing towards more joy can result in leaving old friendships behind, for a while at least.

Often the best way to help someone make choices that might bring them more happiness is to get out of their way. It's about fixing ourselves, rather than anyone else.

Adam and Eve taught us not to talk, trust or feel. How do we break out of those bonds? Honesty in any relationship is a risk. It was one that Shay was committed to take. It mattered to him to be a better role model for Alan. Shay realised that finding a fresh way to deal with stuffed-down feelings was vital for him to find happiness. He attended Beginning Experience; the workshop for separated people which helped him to break the 'don't talk' of his childhood. It's the talking that matters, whatever gets us there. Shay was motivated to find a better way to communicate from the outset of our meeting. Mainly because he knew the ravages of divorce, how sharing kids is not fun. He knew that everything worth having has a cost. It was what made him a great husband; as soon as divorce became legal in Ireland we tied the knot. Unlike many men in relationships, he knew that he couldn't take a moment of our lives together for granted. He wanted to get 'us' right from the start. We were motivated to do our best. Despite that, it could still be paralysing for both of us to show up about certain issues. Fear of him dying broke through any inertia.

Most couples collude with each other, ignoring the 'no go' areas. Shay and I wanted more. We stumbled a lot of the time trying to find it. If Shay was still here in the flesh, what would we be stumbling over? I figure the kids would be our main focus and triggers. Teens bring out the black and white in me. I don't cope very well with the grey of issues such as the children progressing to being young adults. I want to trust that they have what it takes to negotiate this part of their journey but the mammy in me can get a bit frantic. All I know for certain is that I want to keep my children safe. Society suggests that there is a simple black and white formula that equals effective parenting. It involves 'setting boundaries'.

CHAPTER 23

My map of any colour

The boundary we wanted to be able to set for ourselves as a family was to hold off the grim reaper. In the absence of that as an option, what does setting boundaries mean to us? Boundaries imply rules and regulations. Instead I want my children to have 'choice with accountability'. If they learn that every choice has a consequence, then they will have the toolkit needed to make choices that work for them when rules around them are being challenged. It's less telling them right from wrong as opposed to teaching them to discern what will have a better outcome for them. Unfortunately, what they naturally think as 'working for them' doesn't necessarily work for us as parents.

A while ago, It took more than thirty minutes for me to convince Grace that going to her music class was a good idea. Driving away from the class she commented

"It was great, but the only problem now is that you'll do that smug 'I told you so' look."

I tried to listen. It was difficult to put my indignation on hold. So I shut up. Once we got home I invited her brother to add his tuppence-worth, trusting that he might bring a bit more balance to it.

"Yeah, you do the smug thing, but I just got used to it".

I dug deep to apologise. I added that, if I seemed happy, it was that I was chuffed that either of them succeeded when they had doubted themselves. "Nah," they insisted "you are just smug."

I struggled to take this on board.

"How is it that I get to pay for the instrument, the lessons, the petrol getting there, waiting in the cold plus hours of encouraging you to give it a try or to try harder. What am I meant to feel when it all comes together?"

They looked at each other in surprise. It had never occurred to them that I was part of the equation. How do we show our kids that we love them, at the same time as teaching them to value and respect us too?

In my efforts to assure them that my love is unconditional, I have tipped the balance. Slavery is illegal but I have taught them to relate to me in that way at times. It's difficult for them to develop accountability when they feel automatic entitlement. Of course it is wonderful that our children can presume to depend on us to be there for them. But it feels like the job description could do with a bit of a tweak.

We dedicate our lives to giving our children a happier experience than we had. For that to work, we would need to be able to guarantee being a buffer in their lives forever. Shay and I couldn't protect our family. Grace was only months old when everything fell apart for us. We discovered the hard way that trying to make our children's life pain-free only limits the amount of disappointments they know how to deal with.

It often surprises me how unimpressed my children are about experiences that would have brought pure delight for us growing up. The outcome of giving them fewer negatives seems to be to deprive them of an ingredient needed to appreciate positives. With the added element that they have fewer skills to be able to cope when life becomes difficult. There is something about allowing them to feel discomfort alongside comfort, to know in their gut what works for them. Instead of my impulse to protect them all of the time, it's time to let go. To encourage them to discern what their own version of clean truth might look like. This way they learn to value joy at the same time that they develop the 'muscle' needed to keep going in hard times.

It starts with them being accountable for their actions. That means we adults have to be accountable for ours. Years before he was diagnosed, Shay gave Alan an earful about the state of his room. Leaving Alan to clean it up, I brought Shay into our room to remind him of the less than perfect state of it. It was like I had hit him. In our day, no one questioned the adults. It can be hard to reconcile that it is fair game now. I want my kids to be able to question me but not just as a dumping ground. It's about them taking responsibility for themselves, a way for all of us to keep growing.

I want the kids to learn about themselves through honest interaction with others, to be able to discern the difference between constructive criticism and people projecting their stuff on to them. Judgement attacks our identity. Writing this, my lioness hackles ruffle at the idea of anyone attacking my kids. But in truth, I am one of the elements that can put pressure on them to be a certain way when it is not necessarily their truth.

When I am feeling self-conscious, any crap messages about myself that I haven't yet sorted, I project on to them. If I can't look right, then if they look right and seem to be achievers, it suggests to the world that I must be okay. The ultimate accessory. That part of me that needs my kids to make me look good. Gloriously, the only guarantee I have is that they will probably let me down just when I most need them to impress. Deep down the 'mammy' in me knows this is a positive sign of their ability not be defined by me or anyone else. But when they refuse to 'play' by my rules and it makes me look bad, the lesser me wants to throttle them.

CHAPTER 24

Boundaries... hmmm

One of the best ways to unearth what lies deep within us is to go into battle with a teen. What is my biggest challenge trying to parent teens alone? Being good cop and bad cop at the same time without Shay to help me to see what I am bringing to it. Adolescents rarely choose boundaries. It falls to us parents to come up with the goods. Should we become dictators in our kids' lives or is there a gentler way? I need to figure out what I feel about the boundaries myself before I can teach my children. Me, who can't say no to chocolate!

I gave up making New Year resolutions decades ago because I never keep them. Yet somehow, magically, I am meant to be an expert in self-discipline in order to be a half-decent mother. In my day, boundaries were set by hitting us. There were times when I got 'six of the best' daily at school. This poses a challenge in how I am meant to discipline now. Setting limits with my kids feels like one more place to fail as a parent. Am I being too strict or too lax according to society's standards? Teens are never going to welcome boundaries so how do I deal with their resistance?

A few years after Shay died, Grace was angry and asked me to let Shay know. She started from a tame place but soon warmed up.

"Tell Daddy that I am so cross that I would stick sharp pins in his eyes and get an elephant with diarrhoea to pooh in the holes".

Presuming that feelings are better out than in, I tried to trust that this was a good thing but I felt a tad out of my depth. I was struggling to keep composure so as to not seem fazed by her vitriol. Brian came to watch. His nature is such that I imagined if anyone might stop Grace, it would be him. Instead, I saw him grinning in delight as he added his own gruesome contributions. They both waited patiently while I repeated their words in the direction of the ceiling. I kept telling myself that letting out feelings in a safe way is a good thing but I wondered if this image was going to haunt me when they were both going down as axe murderers. After an hour of increasingly hysterical giggles, along with hideously sinister proposals of what Shay deserved for dying on them, they toddled off to bed. I was a wreck. They both remember it fondly. So far, neither has shown any further axe murder tendencies but for that hour I hadn't a clue what was the right thing to do. The culture I was brought up in would never have allowed children to speak with anger towards a parent.

What does it mean to be a good parent? What about boundaries on the expectations of our parenting? This is the only unpaid job that demands 'twenty-four/seven' commitment, minimal training with full responsibility. We try so hard to get it right, to do it right. Sometimes we fail miserably. The clearest measure seems to be when we get it wrong. Boundaries are spoken about more in terms of how our children's behaviour affects others. We are to teach them manners coupled with good behaviour. All the while we are meant to be unconditional in our love. But what about the times when we are not 'feeling the love'? This is not to excuse abusive behaviour, but parents are human. We are often pushed to our limits. It is presumed that we want to treat our children in a respectful way but we need it to be effective too. Sometimes that feels an impossible match. All of my friends admit cracking in some way at some time. They always feel remorse, there is little to be said on the right or wrong of these actions. Admitting that they happen is the first step. Life needs to become real to change.

We spend most of our lives hiding any element of our parenting that might be judged as less than perfect. From licking the corner of our t-shirt to wipe a mucky face, to a friend impulsively buying her son a game-boy en route to the in-laws. The son couldn't believe his good luck. The mum's agenda was to stop him from scratching his backside due to worms. We hide anything we feel might be judged, as parents we are especially ashamed about admitting to 'losing it'. I believe that it is crucial to make it safe for us to talk about when we feel stretched in our parenting. How can we find ways to be assertive and unconditionally loving at the same time? That seems to be the ingredient that could stop us from being either explosive or pushovers. The irony is that our children can be our best teachers in terms of assertiveness. Most children are ace at quiet, clear repetition with no intention of giving in. If they learn from us that screaming or whining works, they add that in too.

A friend planned to have an uninterrupted grown-up meal with her husband. For the previous seven years she had read bedtime stories, brought glasses of water, returned little people back up the stairs with patience. She had read every book on the subject of how to put children to bed. The evening arrived. She had spent a week preparing the children that this was grown-up time. Table set, candles lit, she heard the car turn into the drive. On cue, she also heard the pitter patter of feet on the stairs. She exploded. She marched to the bottom of the stairs and hissed demonically "Not another step."

Seeing a foot raised tentatively in defiance, she leant forward and announced "Straight back to bed or I will break one of your toys."

Having made a wonderful job of breeding confidence into her eldest, he stepped forward trusting that his 'real' mammy was just under the surface of this possessed one. She grabbed the first thing that came to hand, a happy-meal toy (dust covered and faded) that lived amongst the shoes under the coats. She dropped the toy on the ground and, with one clean stomp, smashed it with her foot. Silence. Followed by the children scurrying back to bed. With the added bonus that they never came down unnecessarily at night after that. Where does it say in parenting books 'smash cheap unused toys to ensure family peace and balance'?

Another friend was having a humdinger of an argument with her thirteen-year- old son. After fifteen minutes of a screaming match between them, she attacked him from behind. Grabbing his top, she yanked up his shirt to his shoulder blades. He demanded in indignation to know what she was doing.

"Looking for instructions. Everything else in this house came with instructions."

When Shay was here, each time we faced a challenge we felt taller, happier, more 'grown up'. On my own, some days it feels like I am drowning. I need to figure out my map of how to deal with all of life, regardless of the colour. If our job is to teach by example, it seems to be less about what we do and more about how conscious we are when we are doing it. The decision to take the parental leave when Grace was born was a clear choice for us. We were prepared to live with the consequences. We were not being airy fairy. We had no guarantees at the time as to whether we were making the right choice. Our priorities were different from those around us. To them we were irresponsible, impractical, poor role models. We were financially compromised and intensely happy. With the added delight that, due to tax refunds, we were only half as badly off as we thought we would be. We used to joke at that time "you don't see a hearse with a trailer". We had no idea that two years later, on exactly the same spot in the living room where he had helped to deliver Grace, Shay "died dead". It rendered the parental leave one of the best decisions we ever made.

CHAPTER 25

Grief

There is nothing neat about someone close to us dying. Every cell in our bodies wants to scream in rage, to make the outcome different. It's difficult to capture the experience in words on a clean page, with neat paragraphs. Grief is a visceral and untidy experience. Like a bomb going off in our lives, whatever is closest to the epicentre is what registers first. Initially very little penetrates the aftershock.

A few days after Shay's send-off, I met one of his close friends who had been a tremendous support through the illness. I couldn't remember Dave at the funeral. I presumed there must have been a good reason for him not to be there. I thanked him again for all he had done in the two years before. Later, looking at the footage of the service (we had videoed the funeral for Grace as she was so young), David was reading one of the prayers. I have no memory of that. I must even have been the one to ask him to do it. A complete blank. But ten years down the road, I can still feel the leather of his jacket as I hugged my thanks. I can hear the sound of it against itself, smell the warmth of his kindness. What I am trying to capture is that words have limited capacity when it comes to grief. We feel rather than think the experience. There is something sensuous that is needed to reach past the ice-cold numbness of shock.

I can't do justice to grief and bereavement in words. But I want to challenge any perception of neatness on our part. Years on, it is easy to seem to compartmentalise it. It matters to me that anyone reading this who may be struggling with grief knows that ours was messy and miserable for ages. Missing someone is a measure of how much we loved them. When we deeply love someone, missing them goes on a very long time. Children learn how to deal with grief by watching the way the adults work through it. A widowed aunt of mine offered that all we needed to do was "Eat, sleep and weep according to need for two years."

I liked the simplicity of this. I knew that we weren't going to wake up after two years pain-free, but it made sense that getting back into a family routine would help, allowing sad bits to come and go as needed.

I found weeping in public a challenge. I wanted to let it flow but something would stick every time. It wasn't that I wished to be a permanent waterfall of tears but when an incident cut straight to my core, I wanted to be able to let it go then and there, to only allow it to hurt us once. We had no problem when we were flinging stones on a remote beach or cuddled together on the couch. But walking around places like the supermarket, everything tended to dry up. One day pushing Brian and Grace in a trolley, we passed a perfect lemon meringue tart. Shay had loved them. He would have danced around in excitement having found such a delicious looking one. The kids immediately recognised that this was one of Daddy's favourites. We hovered, wanting to have a reason to buy it. We yearned to be going home to his smile, to watch as he ate his tart with pleasure. None of us were that fond of the taste, so buying it didn't feel right. Just as we were getting over the longing, one of Shay's songs started playing as the background music. The children were swept up in the same wash of pain that hit me. They recognised the song as one Daddy had sung with them in his arms. Instead of letting rip, howling up in the direction of the fluorescent lights and stacked shelves like a family pack of wolves... a few tears slipped down after we had checked that the aisle was empty. We didn't feel safe.

I wanted the children to be able to use this chance to shed their pain but that clashed with my feeling self-consciousness. Yet moments earlier when Grace had let out an anguished wail as her rice cake slipped out of her hands to the floor, no one batted an eyelid. Other shoppers gave us kind, understanding smiles, passing us with no need to fix us or to run away. There was something about the pain of losing Shay rather than a rice cake, that didn't feel easy to release. Because the other shoppers had probably sorted their childhood losses, like dropping food, it meant that it didn't stir much up in them to witness it. But if we let our Shay pain show, their reaction would be based on how sorted they were about the loss, or the risk of losing, someone they loved. It didn't feel like a very safe space to expose the tenderness of our grief.

We thought to wait until we got back home, but we often felt barren and dry by then. Our bodies knew that tears would help but we found it hard to shed them. Brian described it as being like a snail. His tears would collect on his eyelids ready to fall but any distraction made them pull back again, like a wary snail disappearing into its shell. Once retracted, the snail tends to stay firmly inside. Movies continued to help us to melt. We had a special night watching the film "Jack Frost" around Shay's anniversary each year. It felt like our bodies were waiting for it. It's a story about a dad who dies and then comes back as a snowman to say goodbye properly. We clung to each other, laughing at the funny bits and sobbing whenever it matched our memories, holding tight. We would wake next morning puffy-eyed, with a little more peace than we'd had twenty four hours before. Tears had washed away our pain again. We loved when we discovered films that gently nudged us past our resistance. We still do.

Because I knew that the children's map to cope with Daddy going away was watching what I did, it forced me to step up to whatever I could find to work through the bereavement. The pain didn't lessen for us after two years. In fact, we found we were less numb so we felt the agonising rawness more. The emotional blanket that Shay had wrapped around us kept us warm for a time. Just as we were getting properly in touch with our loss, we hit the two and a half year mark. We sensed the time pressure to seem sorted. It sent more of our pain underground. People cared, they wanted to see us happier. They understandably celebrated any time we looked like we were coping. Our pain reminded them of what was buried inside of them too. So it was natural that their greatest enthusiasm was for whenever we looked sorted.

We juggled between looking okay while trying to get rid of our grief behind closed doors. Too much anger and pain got stuffed back down this way. Why? I wouldn't push a thorn back under my skin when nature tries to help it up to the surface. Thorns only happen by accident, if we are unlucky. Yet every human being has had loss of some sort. We need to find ways to be more real about grief rather than pushing the experience back down inside. The Daggara tribe in Burkino Fasa have a weekly 'grief tending' with the same regularity as we'd do a clothes wash. Imagine feeling genuinely clean of sadness and anger on a regular basis.

There is no perfect formula for grieving; it takes as long as it takes. Like a stack of bills waiting for attention, a big part of the anguish lightens once it is faced rather than avoided. Part of my resistance to dealing with it was a fear that if the pain stopped, my connection with Shay would stop too. Dealing with grief has allowed me to bring all that was good between us into my life today while shedding the sadness of us not getting to grow old together. Along the way I heard that seven years was a more realistic length of time to expect grief to hang around. In the absence of a way to fully grieve being a normal part of our culture, it has taken that long and more. I noticed in my seventh year that a deep ache I had come to experience as part of me had lifted quietly away.

My favourite story about grief is of a widow who had lost her hubby two years previously. A bereavement expert whom she had known as a child was back visiting his parents. All these years later, he was considered a top authority on loss. Seeing him on the road, she enquired,

"Do you think he is happy? Do you really think he is happy up there?"

The response was a reassuring "I'm sure he is."

She retorted, "How the f**k could he be, with me miserable here?"

That was the first thing I ever heard about bereavement that made sense to me. Thanks Christy!

It was a hard road. Knowing stuff, like how kids blame themselves, needs a healing that goes further than words too. A few years after Shay died, Grace woke in the middle of the night sobbing.

"I'm sorry (pronouncing it 'sawry') Mammy, it's all my fault, I'm so sawry".

I couldn't stop her tears. It felt intolerable until she did stop. Then my having nothing to say that could convince her she was not to blame became a whole new level of unbearable. Her Daddy was gone. Her Mammy and brothers were sad; it must be her fault.

Words were of minimal use trying to reach her there. Drawing pictures of angry or sad faces, screwing them up into a ball and throwing them against the wall helped. When she had battered the scrunched up ball against the wall enough times for her to feel a little better, we would unravel the sheet to draw a happier face on the back. Grace loved when we went out in the garden to set the crumpled picture alight, sending the sad or happy face up to Shay in smoke. There was something satisfying in the drama of the flame, with the smell of the smoke reaching deep inside of us. Hours playing on the beach seemed to bring her ease as did her hands deep in soil in the garden. The sun or wind wrapped around her also brought a soothing where words did not seem to reach. We are born as part of nature. It gives us the ability to feel, to love, to laugh. It makes sense to go there to heal.

CHAPTER 26

Finding real substance

A little girl playing in the garden is a pretty image. What if I listened to my body, my nature, what if I opted to go feral for a month? Not quite such an attractive picture. This implies that when I listen to nature, it is through the filter of what others find acceptable. Nature doesn't set these sorts of limits. I do. It can take a lot to resist what other people perceive as success. Living in a world full of judgement, I was raised to care about what other people think. The right house, car, clothes, shape, kids, holidays. Somewhere along the way, the message I was given was that if I could tick all these boxes, then I would find peace and joy. If these came naturally I wouldn't say no but so far they haven't, so why do I still accept them as a measure?

I have bought enough 'stuff' to know that it doesn't bring me real joy. Happy in the moment, but it soon wears off. And good feelings that come from my striving to keep people happy are more about me being a successful manipulator, rather than my own core happiness. Smiling and nodding yes at the times when

I actually mean no is a major way that I allow our peace and joy to be undermined. I give my power away so easily. The only person responsible for that is me.

When Shay died, our kids needed both cuddles and stories of what they had done with their Dad. Because Grace was so young she would hear Brian crying that he missed his Daddy to play with and she would join in the crying.

"I miss my Daddy to play with too."

Then looking up she would add,

"Did my Daddy play with me?"

We'd take out all the photos of 'rubbing noses' kisses and visits to the zoo. We piled them on top of unwashed breakfast dishes or whatever was left on the table. We didn't notice or care. All that we registered about the space around us was that Shay wasn't in it anymore. We would push whatever aside to make space to write Shay letters or messages on helium balloons. We'd send them off to Shay. Then we would need time to fling stones into water for all the feelings that had come up. We often found that the plop of stone breaking water didn't quite match the feeling inside. Banging stones together proved more satisfying.

Our favourite became filling balloons with water and then smashing them on the ground. On one occasion, we filled one hundred and fifty ordinary balloons (water balloons can be too fecky to fill). We dragged them in an empty box out to the garden. It was magical smashing the unending supply of them. Squealing and giggling with battle cries as we flung each one into the air. They tend to bounce so there is the added enjoyment of chasing after the intact wobbling balloon, then smashing it with even more vigour. The kids never complained about having to collect up the balloon remnants. It all helped. We would turn back to the house exhausted. Then, when I felt that bed was the only attractive option, they would want feeding again.

We puddled along. Being tidy was irrelevant. I have never obsessed about housework. I try to ensure that we avoid being a health hazard, though we rode pretty close to that too at times. Then someone would visit. Someone who was definitely not a single parent. They tended to be less in touch with their emotional baggage. Standing in my kitchen, they would struggle to contain their worried look for me. Suddenly any sense of us 'getting through this nightmare' would disintegrate into my feeling a total slob. A voice inside would feebly defend my wave of humiliation.

"I am doing the best that I can. I am trying to shift the ache inside instead of pretending it's not there."

Their one raised eyebrow at our chaos could squash the substance of me to almost nothing.

Knowing there was a good chance that someday these critics would have a life experience which might mean they would 'get it' was little consolation. They lived in a world where they believed they could control whatever came their way with a neat cutlery drawer. Despite knowing that this wasn't true, I felt two inches tall. My kids needed a happy, confident, efficient mother. All they had was my inadequate attempts to put our shattered life back together. The polite ignoring of the crumbs on the table by the visitor reminded me that I was delusional if I thought that it was okay that my kids had grubby faces, but we had belly laughed once that day.

These guests meant well. They genuinely cared for our happiness but they measured us by their own value system. It felt like sliding back down in snakes and ladders. Life was crap. I was crap at trying to make it right for our kids. Years later, we all fit back in our skin. In hindsight, it is easy to trust what we did was right for us. At the time, the guilt of failing was a constant knife churning in my gut. Books would urge me to trust my intuition. Then a well-meaning friend would silently tut-tut about my obvious lack of gardening or dusting. The little substance I had to offer my kids would deflate. How do we find the balance to trust our intuition whilst hearing the concern of friends?

Friends can inspire us to push past our limits, to stretch even further. I do believe that living with order is great, but order that comes from the inside rather than fear of other people's disapproval. I'm not saying that I am right and they are wrong. I am asking myself why it is that I automatically feel 'wrong'. The challenge is to own my boundaries, but I feel like a leaf in the wind blowing in whatever direction the strongest force comes from. Some days I felt like the last leaf left on a branch in winter, exposed and raw. I want to get to a place where I hear what my gut has to say more than hearing what others say about me.

About two months after Shay died, I was feeling hopeless. I sat looking at the urn of Shay's ashes. I was crushed that he had left us. We had made a good team and now all that remained was me holding a metal container of ash. Brian loved to look into the urn. We usually waited until Grace was asleep to avoid her seeing it as a personalised sandpit as Shay would probably end up between the floorboards. This day, I was too numb to care. I looked inside for myself. Gracie toddled over from playing. Her tiny hand immediately delved into this different, gritty sand with glee. Her eyes sparkled with delight at this touch sensation. I was torn. I couldn't suddenly pull her hands away and say, "No, this is your Daddy, don't touch."

I knew Shay would be easy about it but it was one of those moments when I had nowhere outside myself to check if this was a good idea. I figured the majority of people would find it creepy and 'wrong' that a two year old play with her Daddy's ashes.

I spread a black bin liner on the floor. Grace sat emptying fistfuls out of the urn. Usually a girl of extremes, she carefully released five handfuls on to the shiny surface. Every so often she looked up at me with a twinkle in her eyes. There is smooth dust in ashes along with minute fragments of bone. Grace spent a long time feeling the grit drop away and the silky texture of what remained on her chubby little fingers. I relaxed. She seemed to sense the specialness of this sand play. We made patterns by drawing our fingers through the scattered ash. The black plastic was a perfect backdrop.

Grace has never done 'feelings' easily. It can be difficult for her to let them come to the surface. But this day after about ten minutes of gentle play, she jumped up to wrap herself around me. Clinging with the childlike wisdom of this being about the pain of Daddy going away, we rocked gently for a time. Gracie started chuckling at the patterns left on my navy sweatshirt by her hands. She patted on more designs. It was weird to have this sort of hug from Shay with the added rationale of an adult that this was more corpse than cuddle. I was getting my head around this while flashing stain removal advertisements, wondering how to make sure I got all of Shay back into the urn, when the doorbell rang. I looked completely ridiculous. Gracie's numerous handprints were perfectly defined.

I stood at the front door talking to a bemused neighbour. Instead of feeling embarrassed, I found that I was trigger-ready to intercept any unconscious impulse on her part to dust me down. My only discomfort was the antennae I had out to Grace being left alone with the urn. When I got back, Grace was sitting, playing quietly with the spiral designs on the plastic. I joined her, we grinned at each other with tangible joy. We couldn't play with Shay the way we wanted to, but this made him feel closer. When I am in touch with the real substance of me, what others think is irrelevant.

CHAPTER 27

Substance?

I want to work out what this substance is about. I suspect that the more I dare to be real, the more it will land. I would love your help. What I am hoping for is friendship that allows space to grow. Good old stretch mark and farting acquaintances. Not for the shock factor but for the ease and space to feel it is okay to be human. Not wasting energy or time trying to be something that I am not. I don't have answers but I am realising that after many hard won lessons, I do have a definite belief system; values that I developed by watching from the back of the class.

I believe that I am a volunteer not a victim. Every moment of my life is a consequence of the choices that I have made. I want to make better choices!

I believe that the best choices I make are when I listen to my body. When I pay attention as to whether something feels 'light' to me. In an effort to stop myself being impulsive, I check in again to see if it would still feel light in five years' time.

I believe that it is not about blame. It's about what happened then, in terms of what is happening now – taking action to move through it. I can't change the past; it only serves as a signpost. Licking wounds can seem satisfying but keeps me locked in misery, a waste of time. Nothing changes. I am hungry for change.

I believe that change happens at the point of action. If we want our lives to be different, there comes a point when we stop talking or thinking about it. We need to get off our ass to do it.

I believe that being able to forgive is vital to health and happiness and a bugger to make happen.

I believe that experience is more valuable than any theory. I love reading ideals about how life can be different, but they stay on the page taunting me unless I can find a way to make them a reality. I don't want to be led by someone who hasn't lived life and had fun in the process.

I believe that farts and feelings are better out than in. Not in a way that causes toxicity for others, but by finding space for our bodies to do what they need to do. Ownership and honesty are my starting point.

I believe that when I avoid dealing with conflict it ends up stuck in the other person. In fact it ends up stuck in both of us.

I believe that we all want to be visible. I love the peace and happiness that I feel when I am seen and accepted for who I really am. Celebrated. It can be daunting to bare all. But even if I am hiding my true self, I still want to be noticed. When I am being a pain in the ass, attention seeking, I am begging to be seen. When I am being creative, I am daring to be vulnerable, daring to show you who I might be.

I believe that we all want to belong. It probably traces back to a survival mechanism in Stone Age times. Feeling different or separate causes us profound pain. I know this drives many of my choices. There is a baseline fear of humiliation or 'outcast' that feeds most decisions I make.

Validation is where I blossom. When I am told that I am loved but my actual experience is to feel invalidated, a quality of insanity creeps into my core.

I believe in hope. When I reach back to the shock of the diagnosis or the bleak emptiness of Shay's dying, I can taste how hopeless life felt then. Breaking free meant facing feelings that my first impulse used to be to avoid. Life feels so much better now. It took courage but it has definitely been worth it.

I believe that hope is a nicer place to live. Staying with the question has a better chance of finding what will work best for me. Answers tell me what worked for the other person.

I believe that we are all hungry to feel love. It can be a scary prospect. We may prefer to opt for a car or a cat rather than human beings, but we all share the same hunger. Love is such a blast when it comes from an abundance rather than a need.

I believe that we are as healthy and as unhealthy as the people we choose to be with. Relationships invite us to strive to be our best. Or they remind us that it can be better to wake up beside an empty pillow rather than the wrong head.

I believe that if someone does it with you they can do it to you. Easiest to see in terms of getting involved with someone who is married. A person who is prepared to cheat on his or her spouse, is capable of cheating on you too. For me it applies to all of friendship.

I believe that secrets keep us sick. Life needs to become real to change. Kids know the truth even when we can't bring ourselves to say it. They need to hear it from us to feel safe.

I believe that kids watch better than they listen.

I believe that I can't make anyone else happy, and they can't make me happy. It's about finding my own happiness, then sharing it. What works best for me is to find ways to be creative and have fun.

I believe that it is better to wait for 'them' to ask the questions before we share what we have found as our answers. How many of us have bounced enthusiastically back to family and friends with some new insight expecting to be celebrated for our brilliance? Instead we've hit a wall of indifference or anger. When we radiate health, people ask questions. It's best to wait until then.

I believe that I need to make my health my priority. This starts by choosing what brings me life, all the time.

I believe that self-esteem and creativity are crucial to my health.

Whenever I daydream about connecting in more authentic ways, it seems wonderful. Then a niggling doubt descends that, human nature being what it is, there may be fireworks. When a group of people get together, it doesn't take long for some to start rubbing each other up the wrong way. What's that about? How can we make it safe for all of us to feel comfortable to take out our substance and shake that booty? I figure the most destructive and limiting element we bring to the table is judgement. Pre-packed judgement of ourselves and others is part of the armour we bring along to keep us safe. A map, so we have a false confidence that we know the territory. What I care about is a deeper knowing. Instead of the black and white of judgement, what about coming with an open mind? Checking everything as to whether it feels genuine or not, then to have the option to walk away from the 'or not' stuff. No judgement. Just listening to what feels right for us.

It's a challenge for me to know what is actually 'me' when I am trying to be real. I automatically judge myself without thinking. When I dress myself, there are so many opinions affecting what I choose to wear, there may as well be a crowd of people in the room. What if the room is similarly 'full' when we meet another person? Deciding what matters before I get to know the real person; shedding judgement before we connect means the potential for more space to play. Judgement is the baggage that causes aggro in the playground. It's the bit that makes the games competitive before we even begin.

What would it look like if we left it at home or left it out of the equation altogether? Breaking the habit of judging myself and others is crucial to the foundation of honest friendship. Judgement doesn't even belong to us. It is given. We weren't born with it; our substance didn't start out with it. Judgement is simply a form of crowd control. In the same way that religion is someone else's faith and we all need to find our own faith, judgement is society's way to impose its version of black and white. It's time for us to shake it off. To kick the ass of any black, white or grey thinking that erodes our joy, to find what feels light to us and to keep our attention there.

CHAPTER 28

Are you up for it?

A few years after Shay died, the kids moved to a Steiner school. One of the ideas behind the approach is that the sense of touch tells us more about us than what we are touching. As I tap my finger on the table, I feel the table but there is a barrier, a space between me and the surface. As I continue to tap I feel the space and then become aware of the substance of my finger. I get that my finger has substance. It feels confident, capable, a good place to test out thoughts before making decisions. That's my finger. How do I get to the substance of all of me? Short of finding a way of banging my whole body on the table...

Our substance is easy to feel in simple, clean moments. Those precious snapshots in time when nothing else matters. When I kept vigil beside Shay's corpse, my head and heart were in a place of gentle, quiet ease about what is really important. It is a deep privilege to be present when someone dies. We spend our lives trying to look right, to have the right 'stuff' so as to live up to all the judgements of us, then we pop our clogs and die. How about we don't wait until then? Let's shed the judgement now, spending time together in our substances rather than in the latest designer gear. This isn't rocket science. It's about people coming together with a commitment to being more genuine. What would be needed to make it work?

Maybe it's something about getting older. Once I got past thirty, I stopped caring so much about what people thought and, bingo! Like some underground movement, I discovered others who didn't want to buy into the judgement either. Nowadays, I rarely get to play in a playground. Usually I am minding wee ones who do the playing. But when I enter a roomful of people, it can feel like the delicious anticipation on the edge of a playground. Bring on the swings and slides! Will it be fun? What will I try first? Will I fall flat on my face? Instead of the hunger to see how high the swing can go, my hunger is to push past the constraints of any judgements keeping me small. If I can dare to be real, then I might come away freed from the questions that feel heavy in my body. Just the thought of that makes me exhale in peace. The intimacy that comes from easy honest connection brings me warmth and joy. I love that.

Daring to be authentic and being seen by others is probably the best place to start to find the right answers for what is important to me now, to access my substance, my core. So I aspire to more than is my experience. This book is the raw bones of what I have figured out so far. I need help to move forward. You have an overview of who I am, if it appeals to connect that would be great. We don't need to agree, it's about being honest that we have 'inner bits'. They don't need to match. What matters is that we want something better than what we have now.

It doesn't mean losing discernment, just the harsh limits of judgement. It means bringing 'real' and 'authentic' to whatever baby steps we can take. All we need is the choice to measure everything as to whether it connects with our substance or not. It can be difficult, because it can press all our buttons when people dare to speak with integrity. I was in a situation recently where the conversation turned to how we avoid feeling humiliated. One woman spoke honestly of how she shifts blame in work. How she tells lies to cover her ass. There were two other women present and their discomfort was palpable. It wasn't 'light' for them but I found it fabulous. It was weighing the woman down so she took it out and owned it. Two people felt better, lighter for the honesty, and two were left struggling with what it meant to them for someone to be that honest. It works, providing no one tries to force their opinion on the other. I would love to think of us being able to make it safe enough for each person to show up exactly as they are.

Most situations where people come together to share in an intimate way involve addictions or trauma. Support groups are wonderful when they are helping people move forward. How do we find that sort of clean connection in ordinary life? It's great to have friends to cry with. It is even more important to have friends to have a laugh with. It's easier to stay with the dramas and miseries of our stories than to get off our butts having learnt something from them, to dare to have the courage to risk being pushed out our comfort zones. We need to figure out what mountains we want to climb and then support each other to give it a go. None of this is new or special. Can we make it happen? Can we allow the space for us to wobble our less than perfect bits, while leaving each other free to make our own choices?

My mate Siobhan, of the 'flabby happies versus hen's arses', had a stroke aged 43. She was told that smoking had contributed. Soon after admission, a young physiotherapist came to assess Siobhan's functioning. Inexperienced of life and certainly of Siobhan's default to find the positive in everything, the physiotherapist announced there was over 90% loss and that the outlook was very poor. As the door handle settled behind the physio, the wellspring of Siobhan's substance erupted. Since the collapse, the paralysed side had seemed to lead the way forward, one half of her body like a premature corpse, inviting Siobhan to give in. Using all the strength of her functioning side, she began flailing, rocking, jerking, pulling drips, flinging the TV remote and screaming incoherently. Eventually, sobbing, exhausted, she fell asleep. The following morning the team were amazed to find that Siobhan had unprecedented return in her right arm. Predicted to be an in-patient and wheelchair-bound for a minimum of six months, she walked out of the hospital after four months thanks to another few cathartic outbursts. The nurses used to watch in wonder, placing bets as to what function would return after each new episode. Today, Siobhan is back working, driving, playing flute.

If I had a stroke, would I seek out Siobhan to help me find my truth? Certainly, but it would still be about my truth no matter how much I want to see others as experts. Siobhan defied the medics and walked free into the fresh air. It then took her a year to give up smoking. Her hard won freedom was spent trying to find ways to have a nifty one, away from the disapproving eyes of friends and family. They chose to care and Siobhan chose to have another cigarette. I was one of the people who probably crowded Siobhan's head when she lay at night, grappling with the issue of whether or how she might quit smoking. Our tut-tutting achieved little. What if her head space had been clear? If we had left it up to her to decide what might help her to feel better, deep down inside? It's more than shedding the judgement, it requires respecting each other's choices. Allowing each other the freedom to make choices; to be free to live or die by the consequences of them. That's my stepping stone to finding what brings me life. Owning my choices while leaving others free to have theirs.

How do you fancy daring to be a bit more honest together? It may simply be stretching your own comfort zone by saying something that you wouldn't ordinarily admit to a mate or partner. It may be talking to a stranger on a bus. Go gently whatever you do. We have enough baggage already. This is about feeling better, not adding to it. I started by saying that I wish this was a dialogue. I'm a novice at all of this but if there is a way to connect, I'm up for it.

If you are looking for somewhere to begin…

Website:
www.maryhadstretchmarks.com/
Facebook:
www.facebook.com/MaryHadStretchmarks?ref=hl
Twitter:
twitter.com/StretchmarkMary
By Post:
Miriam Connor c/o Unit 4, IV36 1BS

Thanks a million,
    Love Miriam x